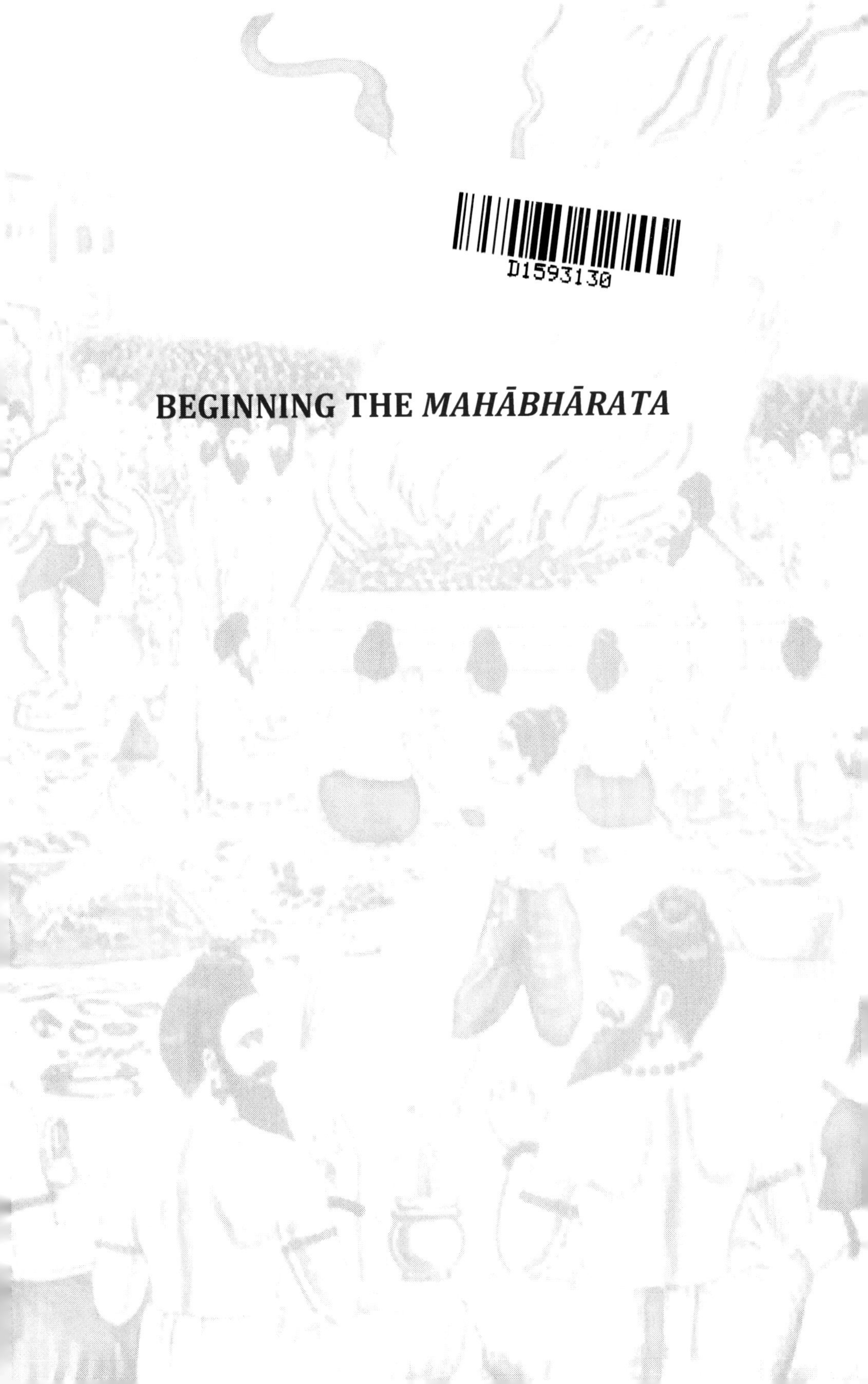

BEGINNING THE *MAHĀBHĀRATA*

BEGINNING THE *MAHĀBHĀRATA*

A Reader's Guide to the Frame Stories

James W. Earl

South Asian Studies Association
Woodland Hills, California
www.sasia.org

Published by SASA Books
A Project of the South Asian Studies Association
Woodland Hills, California 91367
A public benefit, non-profit corporation, EID 26-1437834
www.sasia.org

ISBN 978-0-9834472-2-1
LCCN: 2011944692

Contents

Preface

Anyone who wants to read the *Mahābhārata* in English has a big problem.

First of all, it is so big—some 168,000 long lines, or about twelve *Iliads*. Even more challenging than its size, however, are its complex structure and foreign aesthetic. These make the *Mahābhārata* very, very forbidding for a Western reader. No one could be blamed for finding it simply overwhelming and chaotic. "Oceanic" is a word favored by *Mahābhārata* scholars, probably because that is how the poem describes itself.

It is safe to say that very few Westerners have read the whole poem. There are a few *Mahābhārata* scholars, of course, and we should assume that they have read all of it; their scholarship is extremely impressive, too, but they write mostly for each other. Those without professional training who want to read the poem will find no helpful guidance in print—and helpful guidance is definitely needed.

From the scholarship, one would hardly guess what the experience of reading the poem is like. Scholars do not much discuss their experience of reading it—the effect of its extraordinary length, density, complexity and excesses on them as readers—though they must have spent literally hundreds of hours reading it the first time. Perhaps they were not drawn to it by its literary pleasures and challenges, but by its immense importance in Indian history and culture. Yet the *Mahābhārata* does deliver fantastic literary rewards to anyone who has the patience to take it on, and a big enough appetite for literary and cultural difference. There is no experience remotely like it in English literature—except perhaps *Finnegans Wake*, another book impenetrable without a guide.

What follows is mostly clarification, helpful tips and hard-won summary, with reference to scholarship on critical issues along the way, and interpretive claims of my own, of the sort that literary criticism can best make. Behind the seeming chaos of the narrative, with its innumerable digressions and repetitions, a few great themes are gradually developed which hold the poem together. Among these are the complex relations between ancient India's ruling warrior class and its priestly class (kṣatriyas and brahmins), and the competing claims of violence and non-violence (*hiṃsā* and *ahiṃsā*) associated with them. Only when these themes are clarified can this strange and demanding poem's universal appeal become apparent to a Western reader.

That is one goal of this guide; but it is also intended to be a lively, accurate and accessible introduction to the epic, for anyone with an interest in world literature and the many forms that narrative can assume. The *Mahābhārata* is a truly amazing case. Many passages from the poem are included here, but they barely hint at the qualities of the narrative itself, or the heady intensity of reading it. That is to say, reading this guide is no substitute for reading the poem itself—though it is a good way to start.

Acknowledgements

Many thanks to Dr. Veena Howard of the University of Oregon, and Prof. Adam Bowles of the University of Queensland, for generously reading the work in progress, and to my wife Louise Bishop for constant support.

A Note on Pronunciation

For readers in English, names in the *Mahābhārata* can be confusing enough without the extra problem of the Sanskrit alphabet. Luckily for most English speakers the letters ḍ, ḥ, ṃ, ṇ, ṛ, and ṭ are nearly indistinguishable from d, h, m, n, r, and t; note however that ś and ṣ are both pronounced like English *sh*, and the letter c like English *ch*.

1. Getting Started

Only four unabridged English versions of the poem are available; all others are radical abridgments, paraphrases, or novelizations. Two of the four are by Indians: Kisari Mohan Ganguli translated the poem between 1883 and 1896 in four volumes (4873 pages), and Manmatha Nath Dutt translated it between 1895-1905 in seven volumes (3607 pages). Both translations are in prose; both have been recently reissued, and are available from Amazon.com. Ganguli's is also available on-line, at sacred-texts.com, along with the Sanskrit original.

The third is an American version begun in 1973 by J. A. B. van Buitenen, now being continued by James Fitzgerald. At four and a half volumes it is about half done; it is mostly in prose, with some verse. The fourth translation was recently launched by the Clay Sanskrit Library. Fifteen of a projected thirty-two volumes have appeared, and more are expected (but not all, since the project has been discontinued); all are from the middle of the epic, however.

American readers who want to start at the beginning will certainly prefer the van Buitenen version, with its modern English, excellent introductions, apparatus and notes. After Book I, what is available in the Clay translation is equally attractive; but Ganguli and Dutt are also still readable, and for much of the poem they remain the only choices.

There is another important factor to consider: Ganguli, Dutt and the Clay translators present the "Vulgate" edition of the Sanskrit original (edited in Calcutta 1839, Bombay 1863), which is longer, more detailed, and includes many episodes not found in the "Critical Edition" (Poona 1959) that van Buitenen translates. The Critical Edition is so critical that it is only 146,000 lines long—shorter than the Vulgate by an *Iliad* and a half.

The Vulgate version was compiled from a great number of manuscripts, by the pandit Nilakantha in the last quarter of the seventeenth century. He produced what he called a "thesaurus of excellences" culled from several manuscript traditions. The Critical Edition, on the other hand, is based on a single Kashmiri manuscript of the sixteenth or seventeenth century, written in a script which made it relatively immune to influence over the centuries. Its editor, V. S. Sukthankar, explains,

> While it is the shortest extant version, it is a demonstrable fact that it contains relatively little matter that is not found, at the same time, in *all other versions of both recensions*. It is clear therefore, that it must contain, relatively, *less spurious matter* than any other known version. (xlvii)

It is hard to disagree, but there are good reasons to read both the Critical Edition and the Vulgate, as we will soon see; and since no one but a very serious reader is likely to attempt this project anyway, that is what I recommend.

Between Ganguli and Dutt there is little to choose: Dutt's translation is better formatted and easier to use, but his English is weak, and so is the typesetting; there are literally tens of thousands of errors to distract and confuse the reader. Ganguli's English is better, as is the printing, but one quickly gets lost in unnumbered paragraphs that run on for pages—not a pleasant reading experience.

In spite of these problems, reading Ganguli, Dutt or the Clay version along with van Buitenen adds an invaluable historical dimension to our reading. That is because the Critical Edition presents the *Mahābhārata* as an ancient epic recovered by modern Higher Criticism, shorn of "spurious matter," as Sukthankar says, whereas the Vulgate presents it as a millennia-deep repository of Indian myth, folklore, and cultural tradition. Thus the Ganguli/Dutt/Clay versions expand and elaborate on van Buitenen's with later additions from local traditions, which are interesting in their own right. The relation between the Vulgate and Critical editions is a major topic in *Mahābhārata* scholarship, and reading both will allow us into that discussion.

I also recommend getting an overview of the whole epic before diving in. Without an overview, even this guide may be a little difficult to follow. The just-published Penguin translation by John Smith is the obvious choice. In some 800 pages Smith translates about 11% of the Critical Edition of the poem and provides good summaries of the other 89%. He also writes an excellent introduction for the general reader. There are also usable shorter versions of the epic by William Buck and Chakravarthi V. Narasimhan; each takes great liberties with the original text, but each manages to capture the spirit of the main narrative at least in a single volume.

For an even quicker overview, nothing beats the five and a half hour BBC film of Peter Brook's stage version of the epic. In the case of the *Mahābhārata* it is not exactly cheating to watch a movie of the book, because an immemorial international tradition of performing the epic allows us to accept the film as an interesting variant text. Anyone spending this much time with the *Mahābhārata* will eventually also want to watch at least some of the 72-hour Indian TV version, available on sixteen DVDs. With the *Mahābhārata*, in for a penny, in for a pound!

2. A First Reading

A reader's guide mitigating some of the problems involved in reading such a vast and foreign text should be welcome. Unfortunately, Van Nooten's *Mahābhārata* volume in the Twayne's World Author series (1971) appeared before the explosion of scholarship that followed van Buitenen's first volume (1973); and van Nooten's grip on the poem is extremely loose. Van Buitenen's own Introduction is excellent, but for all his scholarly expertise it contains little helpful guidance for someone coming to the poem for the first time. Hiltebeitel's *Rethinking the Mahābhārata: A Reader's Guide to the Education of the Dharma King* (2001) might appear to be the best recent guide, but it too is written for the scholar; it might just as well be called *A Scholar's Guide.*

I began this guide, initially entitled *Reading the Mahābhārata*, as a memory-aid for myself, but soon realized that even the simplest record would have to be almost as dense and tortuous as the narrative itself. To be useful at all, a guide to the *Mahābhārata* has to be very detailed, because the reader has no choice but to grapple with the poem's myriad intractable details. The poem strongly resists compression.

Well, that may not be one's first impression. Wretched excess would seem to be the rule, and after all, the poem does contain many summaries of itself. Hiltebeitel calls it "collapsible narrative." The more closely we read it, however, the more essential the details seem to be. Most of them are not ornament, but narrative. It is an extremely complex narrative, very taxing on a first reader, but then again the poem was not composed with a first reader in mind. As Ramanujan says, "No Hindu ever reads the *Mahābhārata* for the first time." (419) He compares it, rather, to a language, absorbed gradually throughout childhood.

There are several ways of describing the density and organic wholeness of the *Mahābhārata* that make a first reader's task so challenging. In the opening chapters it is said that one gets credit for reading the whole poem by reading only a single chapter—or even just a summary of a chapter—or one *śloka*—or even a quarter of a *śloka*! (The *śloka* is the poem's basic verse unit, composed of two 16-syllable lines.)

> They who learn even a quarter couplet of the holy study of the *Bhārata*, and have faith in it, will be purified of all their sins. (30)

(I quote van Buitenen and cite his page numbers throughout.) The whole poem, then, is somehow contained in all of its parts, and every part is equally important. That is fair warning that a sequential first reading of the poem will be a vastly diminished reading, because an awareness of the whole is assumed from the very start.

This assumption is apparent even in the poem's frame story: the poem is represented as being presented to an audience of forest hermits who seem already to have heard it before.

> "You speak like your father, boy, we are very much pleased. Your father was always attentive to our wishes—now pray tell this tale as your father used to tell it!" (71)

We, however, have *not* heard it before, so we are at a distinct disadvantage.

The assumption is also apparent in the poem's authorial perspective. Its putative author, Vyāsa, is a mythical figure credited with also having arranged the Vedas and Purāṇas. He has something of the stature of Moses in the Hebrew Bible, or Taliesen in Celtic legend, but as an Indian sage he is virtually immortal and omniscient. In a book devoted to his role in the poem, Sullivan argues that Vyāsa functions in it as a universal consciousness, perhaps even as an avatar of Brahmā. Vyāsa is so central to our reading that Sullivan's book about him will serve as a good general introduction to *Mahābhārata* scholarship (see pp. 13-25 especially).

One of the poem's most unique and puzzling features is that Vyāsa is not the narrator, but rather a character in his own epic. He stands out from the other characters by already knowing the whole poem they are in, which is to say that he sees the past, present and future with a divine eye; and, claiming an author's prerogative, he intervenes in the action more than forty times, like a film director stepping onto the set. Hiltebeitel calls him "the ultimate enigma of his own text": "Vyāsa not only carries his story along. He pops in and out of it like Alfred Hitchcock" (4, 47). Vyāsa encourages the epic's other characters, and the reader as well, to see the narrative as a whole, beyond time. Creating that vision is more important to the work than the literary qualities Western readers are likely to expect, like pace, motivation, suspense and narrative tension; it is a terrible burden to place upon a reader working through the poem chapter by chapter for the first time.

If a reader coming to the poem for the first time knows anything about it, it is probably that it chronicles the dynastic struggle and war between the rival cousins, the Kauravas and the Pāṇḍavas. However, there are some two hundred pages of prefatory materials before that story even begins, which include two interlocking frame stories. These claim to authenticate the poem by documenting its authorship and transmission. Also in these opening chapters there are a number of summaries and tables of contents of the whole poem. Helping new readers through just this part of the poem has come to seem an ambitious enough task, and has the advantage of being achievable; thus my new, more modest title, *Beginning the Mahābhārata*.

This guide, then, will lead the reader through only one third of the first of the epic's eighteen "major books"; slightly more than five of its hundred "minor books"; only fifty-six chapters (sixty-two in the Vulgate) out of over two thousand; only 130 pages of van Buitenen's translation, 123 of Ganguli's, ninety-two of Dutt's. Smith compresses all this material into just ten pages, Buck into seven, Narasimhan into less than five. It is a tiny fraction of the whole poem—about three percent—but still, at about five thousand lines it is a very, very long preamble of a tale, and extremely difficult for a first reader. In his introduction to the poem Smith notes that "the story takes some very unexpected turns in simply trying to reach its own starting point," and calls the opening chapters "frankly confusing, even bewildering." (xlix). Van Buitenen's discussion of them is only two and a half pages long (2-4), and of little use to beginners. We can look forward to returning to it after we have read these fifty-six chapters.

This guide will end, then, right at the beginning of the main narrative—although it is hard to know exactly where that is. Van Buitenen talks about the narrative's "fuzzy edges" and various "perimeters." The perimeter I have chosen to end at is marked by one of the poem's most famous descriptions of itself, as containing everything:

> "Bull among Bhāratas, whatever is here, on Law, on Profit, on Pleasure, and on Salvation, that is found elsewhere. But what is not here is nowhere else." (130)

The choice of this perimeter is somewhat arbitrary, but it happens to be just where Peter Brook's film version begins. Only in chapter fifty-seven does King Vasu spill his seed while hunting in the forest, which leads to the birth of Vyāsa's mother. The Indian television version does not begin until chapter ninety, a hundred pages later.

Reading even three percent of a poem that contains everything requires a good deal of effort, and delivers some of the satisfactions of reading a whole work. That is because these early chapters take us to the heart of major issues like authorship, transmission, oral performance, genre, style, general themes, and the poem's overall structure. Besides, most of these chapters do constitute a whole work, called within the poem *The Epic of Āstīka*.

The guide is aimed at Western readers, and has a distinctly Western perspective. Features of the epic's narrative style that might be unremarkable or even normative in Indian tradition are likely to strike Western readers as highly unusual. For better or worse, it is precisely those features that will most occupy our attention. Our natural concern with the epic's unity, for example, or our attempts to tease apart its intersecting, overlapping and repeating stories, sub-plots and digressions, and determine their relevance to the main story-line, or to try to resolve its apparent contradictions, are almost comically ill-suited to such an encyclopedic, multilayered narrative labyrinth, which seldom proceeds chronologically by cause and effect.

The nearest analogues to the *Mahābhārata* that we have in Western literature are the Bible and the *Iliad*. We will have many occasions to make comparisons to both. The *Mahābhārata* is like the Bible in being composed by many hands over many centuries (c. 400 BCE - 400 CE), in many genres, with many conflicting assumptions and ideas, and yet it comes to us canonized as a single sacred text. Few people read the Bible from cover to cover for the literary experience alone, though it is common enough as a religious practice. Students of literature coming to the Bible for the first time usually start with a close reading of *Genesis*, with the aid of a guide. That is roughly our situation picking up the *Mahābhārata*. It will be good to keep the Bible in mind when we confront issues of unity, consistency and repetition in the epic.

There is no denying that the very idea of reading the *Mahābhārata* from beginning to end, as literature, is a distinctly Western idea, one that the poem does not exactly anticipate or encourage. A critical approach to the poem that proceeds from such a reading will be a sort of thought-experiment, working against the grain to answer the question, What literary experience does the *Mahābhārata* deliver for someone who reads it cover to cover from the beginning? What literary features will we discover? If it sounds like an unlikely approach, it is only because it is untraditional. The modern study of "the Bible as literature" was a similar thought-experiment, and has yielded wonderful results, as we see in the work of scholars like Robert Alter.

Although the Bible is a good analogue, Western literary scholars more commonly compare the *Mahābhārata* to the *Iliad*—a poem normally read from beginning to end, as literature—because it is a heroic epic. In the twelfth century BCE two great battles were ostensibly fought, one on the plains of Troy, one on the field of Kuru. Hiltebeitel speculates (6-7) that the ancient Indian impulses toward both empire and epic might have been provoked by Alexander the Great, who devoutly carried the *Iliad* with him to India on his conquests. Perhaps; but in any case it is illuminating for Western readers of the *Mahābhārata* to keep the *Iliad* in mind while reading, and note how the two poems approach the task of memorializing the battles, the heroes, the roles of the gods, the meaning of history, and the ethics and values of the Heroic Age.

From an Indian perspective, or a purely theoretical one, such a cross-cultural reading may seem a little curious, even misleading. Why constantly compare the *Mahābhārata* to Western works? Not only is the approach necessary, however, but it might actually serve Indian readers too, by "defamiliarizing" a too-familiar text. As an oblique light reveals features of a landscape unnoticed when lit from above, outsiders often see what natives take for granted.

3. Frame Stories

Let us consider the frame stories in a general way before a chapter-by-chapter analysis of them. A surprising complexity assaults the reader immediately upon opening the book.

A frame story is a story about the telling of another story. There are many stories embedded in the *Mahābhārata*—stories for which the *Mahābhārata* is the frame; and the *Mahābhārata* is itself embedded in a frame story about its own telling, which is then embedded in another frame story, about the telling of the first frame story. After only one page our impression is of a bewilderingly complex layering of narrative voices. By the time the main story finally begins, we will be deep, deep inside an 'A said – "B said – '"C said – '"'D said . . ."'"'"' structure, where it may be hard to keep track of who is actually telling the story at any given point.

Many great works of literature begin with frame stories. Chaucer's *Canterbury Tales* and the *1001 Nights* leap to mind. The *Mahābhārata* is not just another instance of the trope, however, for it just might be the mother of all frame stories. Minkowski among others argues that "the *Mahābhārata* is, to a surprising extent, the 'genetic' antecedent of many of the world's best known frame stories." (406)

Because the *Mahābhārata*'s frame stories are about the origin and transmission of the poem, any historical-critical approach to the poem has to focus especially on them. Therefore they have attracted excellent scholarship in English, especially by Fitzgerald, Minkowski, Hiltebeitel, Sullivan and Bowles. Among the many questions these scholars ask are, What can the frame stories tell us about the actual composition, performance and transmission of the poem? And, Is there any history in them?

The poem opens in the voice of an anonymous bard, perhaps the voice of the reader himself, on the occasion of reading or reciting the poem to any audience:

Nārāyaṇaṃ namaskṛtya Naraṃ caiva narottamam ...

The Sanskrit line is taut, balanced, poetic, alliterative, musical—but we will put off Sanskrit for now, and content ourselves with the English:

> The Bard shall intone the song of the Triumph after having bowed to Nara and Nārāyaṇa, supreme among men, and to the Goddess Sarasvatī. (19)

Who is speaking here? It is a voice heard only occasionally in the poem, although in a sense it is the only voice we ever hear. Bowles calls it "the implicit bedrock upon which all other frames are ultimately founded" (163-64). Hiltebeitel calls it "the authorial frame," "an outermost frame that gives the author his openings into the text, and both reveals and conceals its ontology" (34). It was hardly noticed by earlier critics, probably because the narrative's other two frames are so highly developed by comparison, but Hiltebeitel shows how interesting it might be theoretically (92-97). Perhaps, he concludes, the reason Vyāsa is not actually portrayed as reciting the poem, is that the whole poem is already being recited by him. Others disagree (Fitzgerald,"Many Voices," 815-17, and Bowles, 163-64), but the epic is repeatedly described as Vyāsa's "entire thought." As Minkowski says,

> Vyāsa is a transcendent figure in the epic. He is everywhere acknowledged as the author, but nowhere tells the great story. He is the only person in the epic able to appear

> in any level of embedding. He talks to Janamejaya, Dhṛtarāṣṭra, Yudiṣṭhira, and others, entering and leaving the frames as he pleases. (420).

The bard of this outermost frame, then, perhaps Vyāsa himself, begins by telling the story of another bard, Ugraśravas. In the Critical Edition (i.e., van Buitenen) Ugraśravas is called *Sūta*, "the Bard"; in the Vulgate (i.e., Ganguli and Dutt) he is called *Sauti*, literally "son of the bard."

The story begins: Ugraśravas (i.e., the Bard, or Sauti, depending on which version you are reading) pays a visit to the brahmin community of the sage Śaunaka, in the mythical Naimiṣa Forest. (*Pay close attention, this gets complicated quickly.*) Śaunaka and his hermits are in the midst of a twelve-year-long ritual. Śaunaka's hermits welcome the Bard and question him. Their dialogue with him constitutes the poem's first three chapters; in the fourth, Śaunaka himself joins the group, and from that point on the *Mahābhārata* is a dialogue between him and the Bard. "Dialogue" is perhaps not quite accurate, however: Śaunaka asks questions, and the bard's responses constitute the epic. His recitation fills the intervals—the abundant spare time—in Śaunaka's immensely long ritual.

Hiltebeitel calls this setting—the telling of the poem in Śaunaka's hermitage—"the outer frame." Once the main narrative is firmly under way (that is, after the part of the poem covered by this guide), reference to this frame will drop away almost completely, reappearing only fleetingly in the rest of the poem. Smith says, "Aside from a single stray occurrence at 2.46.4, the narration of Ugraśravas the Sūta is not referred to again until the story begins to near its end (15.42-3)." (xlix) Nevertheless, Minkowski argues, "the presence of Ugraśravas is felt throughout the epic." (405)

At first sight, this outer frame hardly seems necessary. What purpose could it serve? Among other purposes, it serves as the frame for another frame; for Ugraśravas (i.e., the Bard, Sauti) immediately explains to his hermit audience that he is not the *author* of the poem he is about to recite; rather, he learned it from the brahmin Vaiśaṃpāyana, who in turn learned it from the author, Vyāsa (also known as Kṛṣṇa Dvaipāyana). On the first page of the epic, the Bard describes for Śaunaka's hermits the momentous occasion when he first heard Vaiśaṃpāyana recite Vyāsa's poem:

> "I was at the Snake Sacrifice of the great-spirited royal seer Janamejaya, son of Parikṣit,
> where Vaiśaṃpāyana recounted all manner of auspicious tales of events, just as they had happened, in the presence of the king.
> They were tales that had first been recited by Kṛṣṇa Dvaipāyana. I myself listened to these stories of manifold import that form part of *The Mahābhārata.*
> I shall speak the entire thought of that great seer and saint who is venerated in all the world, Vyāsa of limitless brilliance.
> Poets have told it before, poets are telling it now, other poets shall tell this history on earth in the future." (20-21)

(I divide van Buitenen's prose into the poem's original *śloka*s throughout.)

As Ugraśravas tells it to Śaunaka, then, the poem consists largely of the reported dialogue between Janamejaya and Vaiśaṃpāyana, in the presence of Vyāsa himself. This telling of the poem at Janamejaya's great Snake Sacrifice is the "inner frame." In this frame it is Janamejaya who asks the questions, and Vaiśaṃpāyana who recites the epic in the course of answering them.

Note that in both frames the auditor (Janamejaya in the inner frame, Śaunaka in the outer) plays a large role in shaping the performance, by asking questions. This will also be true in the many frames within these frames. The *Mahābhārata* is a very *interactive* epic. There is a similar frame in Peter Brook's film version, too: a modern Indian boy asks the questions, and Vyāsa leads him through the story in response. This question-and-answer frame makes the *Mahābhārata* unique among epics. In *The Iliad* and *Beowulf* the main action is presented primarily in relation to a past anterior to it, which appears in inset digressions. The future barely exists. In the *Mahābhārata*, on the other hand, we are never allowed to forget that the action of the poem has had consequences for the future that the audience inhabits. Our future is the frame for the action.

Note too that both the inner and outer frames present the poem as being recited by a visitor during the intervals in a long ritual, or "session" (*sattra*: a sacrificial ritual which takes twelve days or longer to perform). Śaunaka's *sattra* lasts a record-setting twelve years; Janamejaya's Snake Sacrifice (*sarpa-sattra*) lasts a year (Minkowski 413). According to Minkowski, the epic's very structure is derived from the "session," with its vast symmetries, liturgical repetitions, and embedded sub-sections. Another feature of *sattras* seems to be that they provided occasions for telling heroic stories. Thus the *sattra* setting is appropriate for the poem—and yet, a frame story of a *sattra* in a frame story of another *sattra* is oddly redundant. It will take some time to explain its implications.

Homer scholars speculate that a possible setting for a poem the size of the *Iliad* might have been a long religious festival where it could have been told over the course of several days. The case of Greek drama makes the theory at least plausible. We know that by the sixth century BCE the *Iliad* was being performed at festivals, although we do not know if it was actually composed with that in mind. Homer scholars are surprised to learn that this is precisely the scenario described in the *Mahābhārata*'s frames (surprised, because not even Homer scholars read the *Mahābhārata*). Perhaps these frames add some weight to the theory of a ritual setting for the Homeric poems.

The story of Janamejaya's Snake Sacrifice is extremely interesting in itself, and its use as the inner frame will turn out to be important to the interpretation of the whole epic. Unlike the outer frame of Śaunaka's forest ritual, this one is maintained throughout the poem. "The attention of the reader is returned to Vaiṣaṃpāyana and Janamejaya at transitions in the story" (Minkowski, 403). We are almost always aware of the two interlocutors, though the scene of the Snake Sacrifice itself will be evoked in detail only twice, both times toward the end of the epic (15.43 and 18.5), to provide closure.

What makes the Snake Sacrifice a particularly appropiate setting for the telling of the *Mahābhārata*? The most obvious answer is that when we finally get to the main narrative, it will turn out to be a story about Janamejaya's ancestors, especially the generation of his great-grandfather Arjuna, whose grandfather turns out to be Vyāsa himself. Vyāsa, who is present at the Snake Sacrifice, is not only the author of the poem being recited there, he is a participant in the events it recounts, a progenitor of most of its main characters, and Janamejaya's great-great-great-grandfather too. He is author, begetter, actor and lone survivor of the story he tells, a supernaturally long-lived seer who plays a shaping role before, during and after the events of the main narrative.

There are other links too between the main narrative and its setting at the Snake Sacrifice. They will be discussed when we get to the sacrifice itself, which occupies some fifty chapters. For now, we are still on the first page of chapter one.

For clarity, let us summarize the complex layering of narrative voices we find at the beginning of the poem: an anonymous bard tells us...that Ugraśravas told Śaunaka...that Vaiśaṃpāyana told Janamejaya...that Vyāsa told him...and there will be more boxes inside those boxes. Two other dialogues are embedded in the first chapter alone. Minkowski memorably remarks of this Chinese-box technique,

> The reader is presented with a curious narratological question—how can the *Mahābhārata* itself describe the history of its own narration? Or more specifically, if Vaiśaṃpāyana is telling us the story of the Bhāratas, then who is telling us about Vaiśaṃpāyana? ... The *Mahābhārata* provides its own answer. It adds a second narration that tells us about the first one ... But this seems to be a very dangerous solution, since it must necessarily provoke the same question it is designed to answer, now compounded with the threat of an infinite regression. (404, 406)

What is the purpose of these frames? Does it make much of a difference who is speaking at any given moment? Western readers will think of Plato's *Symposium, The Canterbury Tales* or Conrad's novels as classic examples of complex frame narratives in which distance, irony, contradiction, voice, differing points of view and unreliable narrators complicate the reader's responses and interpretation. The frame-narratives and multiple voices in the *Mahābhārata*, however, seldom function in this way. Rather, they add a sense of historicity, assert the reliability of the text's transmission, integrate the poem's many diverse sources (Bowles, 155-90), provide a pretext for adding peripheral materials to the main narrative, and deploy complexity for its own sake as an aesthetic feature. They also announce certain major themes of the poem as a whole.

That the various narrators do not differ from each other in the way Chaucer's do is not to say that they do not differ, however. They just differ in ways we might not expect from Western analogues. The most important difference between them is that the narrator in the outer frame, Ugraśravas, although he is not himself a kṣatriya, (i.e., of the ruling warrior class), serves that class as a charioteer/bard, whereas the inner frame narrator, Vaiśaṃpāyana, is a brahmin (i.e., of the priestly class). Van Buitenen asks,

> Why should these priests, going about their ritual concerns in a remote forest, be concerned with the warlike doings of generations of kings? ... [Also,] it is doubtful whether [Janamejaya] would have been interested in all the brahmanic stories that now have their place in the epic. (xxii)

That is, the poem's main plot has to do with dynastic struggles and war, which are kṣatriyan themes; but the poem is also replete with stories about vows, curses, austerities, sacrifices, ritual purity, gurus, and other brahmanic themes. It is hard not to see these two sets of themes as being in some sort of tension.

Biardeau expresses this tension as a complementarity which is central to the structure, meaning and purpose of the *Mahābhārata*.

> If Brahmans on the whole are priests officiating for generous patrons, the patrons are usually Kshatriya kings. These kings certainly are warriors and wielders of force, of daṇḍa, but as actors in the ritual context of the brāhmaṇas, they first appear as the typical yajamāna, the sacrificers without whom practically no solemn sacrifice would take place. This is a first aspect of the complementarity of the brahman and kṣatra which shows that one could not exist without the other. A priest must have a patron, a patron must have priests, and if their common sacrificial activity were not performed regularly according to prescription, the order of the three worlds would be so upset that it would lead to destruction. (75)

Van Buitenen, on the other hand, concludes from this tension that the story Vaiśaṃpāyana tells Janamejaya is an older, more original, kṣatriyan form of the epic, and that the frame in which it is retold by the Bard to Śaunaka adapts the older epic for a brahmanic audience. Van Buitenen is not at all happy with this brahmin retelling of the story, either, calling it "inept," "silly," and "foolish," among other things (xix-xxi). This "brahmanization" theory is a common reading of the poem among *Mahābhārata* scholars, although it has recently fallen out of favor as too simple to account for all the evidence. Whatever the case, the poem certainly does combine both sets of themes, and combines them so thoroughly that they cannot be separated. Note, for example, that the kṣatriya king Janamejaya hears the story from the brahmin Vaiśaṃpāyana, while the brahmin Śaunaka hears it from the non-brahmin bard Ugraśravas. Obviously a good deal of effort has gone into this criss-crossing super-structure.

Why is this class difference so important to the epic? The nearest analogy in Western literature is in the epics of the

Middle Ages. When oral tales of kings and war, originally secular, passed into writing, they necessarily passed through the monastery, the center of literacy and book-production in the Middle Ages. In the process they were Christianized to some degree. *Beowulf* is a famous, much-debated example. Another is the King Arthur cycle, which over the centuries accumulated more and more religious elements like the Holy Grail stories. There is nothing surprising in the influence of a learned and literate religious class on works that emerge from secular oral traditions.

In the frame narratives of *The Mahābhārata*, however, brahmanic influence is not only acknowledged, it is made one of the chief themes. Some, like Biardeau, would say it is the chief theme. Fitzgerald puts it this way:

> As the written text presents itself to all its audiences through the ages, the royal audience which was the primary audience of the text, itself became part of the greater text which is attended to by the brahmans, who, as audience for Ugraśravas' rehearsal, themselves became part of the greater text presented to Indian audiences and, eventually, to us. ... Vyāsa's "Vedic" instruction of Janamejaya on his proper action in the world, and the brahman community's monitoring of that instruction represented *the ancient Indian complementarity between brahman and kṣatra—transcendent wisdom and governmental power.* (165, 169, emphasis added)

That last formula, *the relationship between transcendent wisdom and governmental power,* is worth the extra emphasis. That is a theme any reader can relate to, and we will return to it.

4. The Summaries (Chapters 1-2)

After announcing the frame settings, the first two chapters proceed to summarize the whole epic in advance—not once, but several times.

Ch. 1 (The Lists of Contents). Asked to recite Vyāsa's poem, the bard Ugraśravas (Sauti) begins with a quick account of the Creation of the universe from Brahman in the form of an egg, then Vyāsa's life, and then the creation and transmission of the poem. We learn that Vyāsa composed a Bhārata (the epic without its many sub-plots) in just 48,000 lines, and also a summary of it in just 300 lines. He also composed a version with over a *million* lines—only 200,000 of which, however, were intended for mankind. That is the version—famously 100,000 *śloka*s—that he taught to Vaiśaṃpāyana. Is that the poem we are reading? If so, somehow it manages to include its own frame stories, which describe its future transmission before the fact. That sort of brain-teaser will be typical of the poem.

In the Vulgate version of this opening passage we find one of the poem's most popular details, already familiar to us from Brook's stage and film version, the charming story of how the elephant-god Gaṇeśa was enlisted as Vyāsa's scribe. It is told in embedded dialogues between Vyāsa and Brahmā, then Vyāsa and Gaṇeśa. It is an important story, too, since it reports the passing of the epic from oral into written form, and identifies difficult and contested passages in it; but the Critical Edition does not include it. That is the sort of thing we miss in reading van Buitenen. Fitzgerald says,

> This small addition to the text was an ingenious and persuasive way to bring the manuscript tradition of a profoundly disturbing text under the benevolent aegis of the

> god Gaṇeśa, and if it had occurred to the redactors or promulgators of the fixed, written Sanskrit *Mahābhārata*, the text [might] have had a somewhat different, less clouded history. (156)

That is, ironically, the Critical Edition is less conscious of its literate textuality than the Vulgate is.

After these preliminaries, most of chapter one consists of a "list of contents" of the whole poem. The first part of the summary (from the birth of the Pāṇḍavas to the episode of the dice game) is told by the Bard; the rest is presented by him as a dialogue between two characters, Dhṛtarāṣṭra and Saṃjaya, after the great battle. Here is yet another of the poem's many frames: much of the epic—as readers of *The Bhagavad Gītā* already know—takes the form of Saṃjaya responding to Dhṛtarāṣṭra's questions. The entire battle (Books VI-IX) is narrated (largely in retrospect) in that frame, the most elaborately developed frame in the whole poem (Minkowsky 406). It is a very nice literary touch that the summary of that part of the poem, here at the beginning, is cast in a similar frame.

As a narrator, Dhṛtarāṣṭra is certainly closer to the action he is recounting than Janamajaya and Śaunaka are, four generations later, but being blind, he too has learned about it only by listening, mostly to Saṃjaya. Having heard it all, here he tells it back to his teller in his own way. His list of episodes foreboding disaster is certainly a striking technique for summarizing the epic in prospect/retrospect. Its repetitions remind us of the epic's oral style, easily forgotten as we read our English prose translations.

> "When I heard that Yudiṣṭira had been defeated by Śakuni Saubala in a game at dice and was divested of his king-

> dom, yet still was followed by his inscrutable brothers—then, Saṃjaya, I lost hope of victory.
>
> When I heard that Draupadī, tears in her throat, had been dragged into the assembly, grieving, in a single garment, and she in her period, while her protectors stood by as though she had no one to protect her—then, Saṃjaya, I lost hope of victory..." (25)

Fifty-five episodes are listed in this way in van Buitenen's translation—although there are sixty-six in Ganguli's and Dutt's. According to the numbers provided right in the text of chapter two, Book I in the Vulgate is almost 1800 lines longer than it is in the Critical Edition. In chapter one alone, the Gaṇeśa story and Dhṛtarāṣṭra's list account for some of the difference. Let us pause for a moment to compare the two lists. All fifty-five episodes in the Critical Edition's list appear also in the Vulgate's, although there are a few changes in order; and episodes which are added in the Vulgate's list refer not to added or minor episodes in the poem, but to important ones that also appear in the Critical Edition—for example, the stripping of Draupadī, inserted right after the item quoted above.

> "I had no hope of success, O Sanjaya, when I heard that the wicked Dushasana had been able to drag out only a heap of clothes without finding its end when he had attempted to strip her of her single cloth." (Dutt, p. 7)

(Ganguli's and Dutt's summaries, by the way, are nearly identical; they differ by only a single item, and a few changes in order.)

What do we learn from this comparison? In the end, the Vulgate's list of episodes seems more complete and faithful to the shape of the poem, and by comparison the Critical Edition's seems awkwardly truncated. It is easy to see why one might prefer the longer version, and one begins to wonder about the editorial principles that yielded the Critical Edition by including only passages that appear in all manuscripts. Sukthankar, the editor of the Critical Edition, is quick to admit that the Vulgate

> will appear in places, at first sight, to be even "better" than the critical text, because the former has been purged [sic] by the continuous emendations of scholars for centuries. A whole army of anonymous scholars and poets must have worked at the text to make it smooth and easy of comprehension, and to increase its popularity and usefulness by adding to it interesting anecdotes, incorporating into it current and popular versions and explanations, bringing it in a line with the ethical, moral, religious and political ideas of essentially different ages. (ciii)

But is an earlier, shorter version of a work necessarily more authentic? The same question arises in biblical studies: for example, should we consider the "J" document more "genuine" in some sense than the final redaction of *Genesis*? Scholars disagree, but today most say no. The final version is no less authentic, and is in some ways moreso.

At the end of his powerful, if formulaic, summary of the poem's action, Dhṛtarāṣṭra realizes that all of his sons (and millions of others) have died, and he decides to kill himself. Saṃjaya dissuades him, arguing that all those who died would have died anyway. His argument has a personal side and a metaphysical one:

> "Your sons were wicked and consumed with rancor, greedy, mostly evil in their ways—you need not mourn them...
> Time ripens the creatures. Time rots them. And Time again puts out the Time that burns down the creatures.
> Time unfolds all beings in the world, holy and unholy. Time shrinks them and expands them again.
> Time walks in all creatures, unaverted, impartial. Whatever beings there were in the past will be in the future.
> Whatever are busy now, they are all the creatures of Time—know it, and do not lose your sense." (30)

This is the first statement of the poem's major theme. From a Western point of view, and from an Indian one too, the theme of Time as the great destroyer is devastatingly negative. In a nice understatement, Shulman calls it "the somewhat austere vision characteristic of puranic cosmology."

> This lament, which concludes the introduction to the text and the initial synopsis of the story, will recur almost at the very end of the epic, in the Book of the Setting Forth (17.1.3), when the Pāṇḍava heroes, having survived the apocalyptic battle, and having witnessed the deaths of their own sons, abandon the world and begin their long walk up to heaven. We might, in fact, regard this whole epic as an extended essay, carried along on a complex narrative frame, on time and its terrors... To this day, this text is not recited (or even stored) inside a house, lest it consume the building and its inhabitants... The *Mahābhārata* is fire, never wholly contained by the accumulation of frames that bind it. (26-27, 29)

Fitzgerald too notes that the epic "has long been regarded as an inauspicious text" which "is not read or recited in their homes by pious Hindu people." (156)

Ch. 2 (The Summaries of the Books). Now the poets get *really* serious about summarizing the poem. After a mythical history of the battlefield itself, and a numbering of the eighteen armies destroyed in the eighteen-day battle to be recounted in the epic's eighteen books, the whole poem's contents are summarized twice more. Those who do not like summaries should stick to van Buitenen's translation, because the Ganguli/Dutt version of this chapter is almost twice as long—but also twice as interesting. Even the opening story of the battlefield is more interesting in the Vulgate, for being developed in dialogue between Rāma and his ancestors.

This is the battlefield where the eighteen armies of the Kauravas and Pāṇḍavas are destroyed, at the end of the last age and the beginning of this one. At the end of the *previous* age, we are now told, a similar carnage took place on the same spot:

> During the juncture between the Age of Trey and the Age of the Duce, Rāma, greatest of swordsmen, urged on by his rancor, destroyed over and again the baronage of the earth.
>
> When he, lustrous like the fire, had annihilated the entire nobility with his own might, he made five lakes filled with the blood in Samantapañcaka.
>
> In those lakes with their waves of blood he, insensate with rage, offered up bloody oblations to his ancestors, so we have heard. (32)

This is not the Rāma of the *Rāmāyaṇa*, but another hero, Paraśu-Rāma. He plays a big role in the *Mahābhārata*. Scholarship on this story and related ones throughout the poem is very thick. Paraśu-Rāma is the bloodthirsty warrior-hero of the Bhṛgu (or Bhārgava) clan. What makes him especially interesting is that while the Bhṛgus are brahmins, they are warlike, like kṣatriyas. Rāma is famous for the genocidal wars in which he exterminated twenty-one successive generations of kṣatriyas (translated "barons" or "nobility" by van Buitenen).

According to the Critical Edition's editor, Sukthankar, the *Mahābhārata* is suffused with this Bhṛgu mythology. He proposed the controversial theory that the original kṣatriya epic was thoroughly revised not just by brahmin but by Bhṛgu redactors—that is, that the *Mahābhārata* is a Bhṛgu epic. Whether or not that is the case, the extermination of the kṣatriya class to restore *dharma* is indeed a governing theme in the whole poem. Goldman argues in a book on this theory that the Paraśu-Rāma story was invented precisely for the *Mahābhārata*:

> The Rāma complex is the end result not of a real war or campaign of genocide, but of a mythic tradition of Bhārgava-kṣatriya tension, centering around a struggle for status and a strong uncertainty as to the proper varṇa [class] of the Bhṛgus. Thus the Bhārgava sages assert the Brahmanical prerogatives by means of the weapons of the warrior. (143)

Thus the Bhṛgus can be seen as a clan on the borderline between brahmin and kṣatriya, in a sense unifying them, resolving the conflict. We will learn in chapter fifty-eight that each time Rāma exterminated the kṣatriya men, brahmins fathered the next kṣatriya generation on their women:

> The baronage was begotten on the baronesses by austere brahmins... All four classes were thereafter headed by the brahmins. (136)

However we look at it, the story of Rāma certainly displays the paradoxical complementarity of the two classes: it is the responsibility of brahmins to correct the excesses of the kṣatriyan rulers, but can they do so without adopting those very excesses? In chapter four we will discover that Śaunaka himself is a Bhṛgu, and that the Snake Sacrifice too has strong Bhṛgu elements; and in Book III, improbable as it sounds (for he lived in a previous age), Rāma will enter the plot directly, first of all as Karna's teacher, and later in other roles. There will be more to say about this Rāma, but first we must get to those two summaries in chapter two.

First the epic's hundred "minor books" are listed. The division into a hundred books is attributed to Vyāsa himself. Then, in just eight pages, the contents of the epic's eighteen "major books" are summarized in some detail. The division into eighteen books is attributed not to Vyāsa but to the Bard, Ugraśravas. Obviously two textual traditions have come down to us, and both have been retained as canonical. The narrative remains unaffected by these differing divisions, but they do result in bewildering sets of book, chapter and *śloka* numbers throughout. To make things worse, the various versions available to us are divided somewhat differently. For example, van Buitenen's version of Book I contains 225 chapters, Ganguli's 236, and Dutt's 234. Van Buitenen helpfully provides a table of correspondences. It comes in very handy when trying to find a parallel passage in the Vulgate.

The second summary, that of the major books, is especially interesting. Detailed as it is, however, first readers will not be able to make heads or tails of it, because it assumes that we already know the whole poem. It seems to be a mnemonic device to help bards keep track of the poem's myriad episodes; it even includes the number of chapters and *śloka*s in each book.

As before, it is hard to resist comparing the two versions before us. If we limit the comparison to just the summaries of Book I itself, this is what we find: the summary in the Critical Edition covers Book I in just twenty-three *śloka*s; the Vulgate's summary is exactly twice as long. Once again, everything in the Critical Edition's summary appears in the Vulgate's, but the Vulgate begins with a summary of the summary, and *śloka*s are added here and there throughout. As before, most of the additions refer not to new episodes, but to important ones that also appear in the Critical Edition, for example the Śakuntalā story, and Arjuna's winning of Draupadī. And as before, it is hard not to feel that the Critical Edition is deficient in some way.

It is startling to realize that in both versions of the summary, the fifty-six (or sixty-two) confusing chapters covered in this guide are summarized in just four *śloka*s. One is always surprised by such reminders of the epic's huge scale. Here are the four *śloka*s:

> The summing up of *The Bhārata* is given there as *The Summary of the Books*. The *Pauṣya* glorifies the greatness of Utanka.

> In *Puloman* the ramifications of the lineage of the Bhṛgus are described. In *Āstīka* the birth of Garuḍa and all the Snakes,
> the churning of the milky sea, and the origin of Uccaiḥśravas. Then the story begins of the great-spirited Bhāratas
> as told to the king, the son of Parikṣit, when he was offering with the Session of the Snakes. (36)

Why does the epic begin with more than twenty pages of summaries—in Ganguli more than thirty? Perhaps the ancient poets, acknowledging the epic's oceanic scale, provided us with something of a reader's guide in their own way. Chapter two ends with this dubiously comforting simile:

> When they have first heard this great, incomparably rich epic as it has been laid out in *The Summary of the Books*, it becomes for all men as safe to plunge into as the wide ocean is with the aid of a boat. (44)

As we shall see, summaries are an elemental feature of *The Mahābhārata*'s structure. Long narrative units in the poem are typically introduced in summarized versions, which then provoke an interlocutor to demand a fuller, more detailed version. Without these summaries we would quickly get lost; with them, we feel as if we are going around in ever-widening circles—but at least we have a boat on this ocean!

5. The Snake Sacrifice

As if all these summaries were not odd enough as the beginning of an epic, the chapters which follow them are even odder. They dilate hugely upon the frame-setting of Janamejaya's Snake-Sacrifice. It was during the long intervals in this ritual that the Bard first heard *The Mahābhārata*; but the many stories he tells about the sacrifice itself seem only tangentially related, if at all, to that story, which they delay by an astonishing eighty pages of interwoven myths, forking legends, and meandering snake-lore. Minkowski says of the frame narrative that it is "the most complete compendium of Indian snake-lore that we have in Sanskrit literature." (416) Perhaps all these Snake stories are just later accretions, or perhaps they bear some relation to the main narrative, to be discovered later. There are some interesting suggestions in recent scholarship, especially by Minkowski, Hiltebeitel, Sullivan and Shulman. We will get to them soon.

Even if the Snake stories seem less than necessary to the epic, still they are central enough to have made it into the Critical Edition. They are certainly a dramatic instance of the aesthetic governing the whole poem: digressive, associative, agglutinative, excessive. Imagine Chaucer beginning *The Canterbury Tales* not with short portraits of the Canterbury pilgrims at Harry Bailey's inn, but with an account of Harry Bailey's genealogy, the history of England, the founding of London, the building of the inn, and long biographies of each pilgrim; then imagine twenty or thirty generations of poets adding layers, episodes and digressions to this already distended prologue. That is our first impression of these chapters of the *Mahābhārata*. A closer reading, however, makes all of it seem not only delightful, but somehow necessary.

What exactly is the Snake Sacrifice? It is an *ad hoc*, immense, year-long ritual in which Janamejaya attempts to exterminate all the Snakes in the world. ("Snakes" is capitalized because in addition to real snakes the word *Nāga* refers to a class of common demons that take human or other forms.) Since there are still Snakes in the world, the sacrifice obviously failed. These stories explain, then, first of all, why Janamejaya wanted to destroy the Snakes, and second, why he failed, how the Snake-seer Āstīka managed to interrupt the sacrifice at the last moment. These two intertwining plots extend backwards virtually to the Creation. A lot of mythology is presented in the process, almost none of it pertinent to the main story of the *Mahābhārata*, and much of it just as irrelevant to the story of the Snake Sacrifice. Economy, logic and unity are nowhere in evidence.

That puts the case a little too negatively, perhaps, for the narrative is nothing if not intense, exuberant, flamboyant, clever, intricate, baroque, various, amusing, and often just overwhelming in conception and representation. Once we grasp it, we would not want it any other way.

Much of the story in these opening chapters is presented in reverse. That is, the Bard recounts an episode, Śaunaka asks for clarification, the Bard supplies the requested background, Śaunaka requires further amplification, etc.—creating a set of nesting, ever-receding narrative horizons. In film-language we might say that we keep getting more and more back-stories. Even the back-stories have back-stories, just as the frame has a frame. There is no necessary limit. More back-stories can be added until the poets reach whatever level of complexity they require to portray the causality underlying the main plot. The plot is everywhere vastly overdetermined: an event has many causes, not just one. These techniques, along with the use of summaries, result in smaller and larger cycles of repetition and amplification throughout. If we are patient enough with the process, we come to sense an ever-deepening narrative, with an ever-deepening mythical and legendary causality underlying its ostensibly historical events.

Because the story of the Snake Sacrifice is told at the beginning of the epic, it is easy to think of it as a preface rather than as a frame, but we should keep in mind the frame's temporal dynamics. These early chapters describe the Snake Sacrifice right up to its horrific climax and surprise ending; yet we have to imagine the whole poem that follows it being recited bit by bit during its intervals. Snakes will be pouring into the fire as the apocalyptic battle between the Pāṇḍavas and Kauravas is being recounted; and Āstīka's intervention to save the Snakes will correspond with the ending of the poem. That is, the frame-audience is experiencing its own drama as the main narrative is being told to them, and the themes of these simultaneous narratives reflect each other. As Shulman puts it,

> This work was recited, so we are told, in the intervals of a great sacrifice aimed at destroying all the world's serpents; between chapters or sections, the sacrifice went on. One tells the story in the midst of sacrificial destruction, a ghastly process of violence that is always in some sense primary to the text, providing its proper setting as well as a symbolic restatement of its themes... Vyāsa fathers an entire universe and watches it *consume itself in fire*; the frame shares the general process enacted by the main epic story, within which the listener or reader is also entirely subsumed. (29-30)

Just how does the frame "share the general process enacted by the main epic story"? They are connected because the Bhārata war itself is repeatedly described in the poem as a *sattra*—in this case a "battle sacrifice" (*raṇa-sattra*) in which warriors are offered up, as Snakes are offered up in the *sarpa-sattra*. Once we are aware of this important symbolism, the frame story becomes powerfully relevant to the main narrative. Now we have the story of a *sattra* being recited at a *sattra*, being recited at another *sattra*. The parallels between these sacrifices will figure large in our eventual conclusions.

Because the *Mahābhārata* is first told at the Snake Sacrifice, and because Janamejaya is the sole direct descendant of the Bhārata line which the epic celebrates and eulogizes, we may not notice at first that the story of the Snake Sacrifice amounts to a sharp brahmin critique of him as king. Janamejaya is not being offered to us as an unambiguous hero, or simply as the inheritor of Bhārata glory. Rather, in wanting to exterminate the Snakes he is acting too much like a kṣatriya and not enough like a brahmin—from a brahmin point of view, of course.

As a kṣatriya, Jamamejaya needs brahmins to conduct the sacrifice. They are not in a good position to refuse him, but in the end they do prevent him from succeeding in exterminating the Snakes. As a kṣatriya the king possesses worldly power, and his brahmins possess spiritual power. According to themselves, at least, brahmins are the higher class, and their power is infinitely greater than the king's, but in practice the relation between the two classes is complex. The same was true in the medieval West: consider the struggle between Henry II and Thomas Beckett, or Henry VIII and Thomas More. Eternity is one thing, but in the play of history, how can the Church ever stand up to a king?

Hundreds of the stories in the *Mahābhārata* revolve around these issues. Not only the story of the Snake Sacrifice, but the entire epic can be read as a brahmin critique (and then rehabilitation) of the kṣatriya class. Hiltebeitel calls his reader's guide *The Education of the Dharma King*, by which he means a *brahmin* education of the king. Biardeau reads the epic's great Bhārata War as a brahmin sacrifice of the kṣatriya class, in the kṣatriya class's own interest—

> a sort of Vedic "sacrifice" of the decadent moral and social order (*adharma*) for the rejuvenation of society and for the establishment of a new path to salvation for the warrior caste (in particular the king). (Woods, 10)

The chief themes of this critique, or education, or sacrifice, are (1) the necessity of maintaining clear distinctions between classes, and (2) the dangers of cruelty, anger and violence, which are the characteristic moral failures of kṣatriya life. Kṣatriyan *hiṃsā* (violence) is addressed by a brahmin ethic of *ahiṃsā* (non-violence). But, one has a right to object, how could an ethic of non-violence possibly apply to *warriors*? Biardeau's answer: non-violence is redefined in the *Bhagavad-Gītā*, specifically for warriors.

> A Kshatriya ... should consider all his actions, including fighting as a warrior, as many sacrifices. In this way he is a yajamāna who never stops sacrificing and the battle as a sacrifice is his own variety of it, for which he is the sacrificer, the priest and the victim... *It cannot be called hiṃsā if this violence is not for the sake of killing but intended as sacrifice.* (93, emphasis mine)

The important theme outlined in these few sentences governs the whole epic, as well as the frame story of the Snake Sacrifice. There are interesting differences, however, between the treatment of the theme in the epic and in its frame. Arjuna's killing is a kind of sacrifice, precisely because he achieves detachment from any violent motive; that is what Kṛṣṇa teaches him in the *Bhagavad-Gītā*. But how detached is Janamejaya? Not very, as we will see. In this interpretation, counter-intuitive as it might seem to a Western reader, the king's *sarpa-sattra*, although it looks like a sacrifice, is actually an instance of *hiṃsā*, violence; whereas Arjuna's *raṇa-sattra*, which certainly looks like violence, actually qualifies as *ahiṃsā*, because it is a sort of sacrifice.

No reading will go uncontested, however: in the introduction to his third volume, van Buitenen spends over forty pages rebutting Biardeau's interpretation (142-84).

That said—and it is a lot to have said so early and so quickly—let us finally read the three "minor books," *Pauṣya*, *Puloman*, and *Āstīka*. The first is one chapter long, the second nine, the third forty. In them we will veer into increasingly strong narrative headwinds. The stories of *Pauṣya* and *Puloman* are interesting in themselves, but they are told primarily to provide more or less essential background for *Āstīka*. They are fairly straightforward and unified; by comparison, *Āstīka* is immense, and immensely complex.

6. *Pauṣya* (Chapter 3)

Unexpectedly, this chapter is mostly in prose. It is only eleven pages long, and the Vulgate and Critical Edition versions of it are nearly identical. Since it is the first extended narrative in the epic, it provides a good opportunity to describe some of the *Mahābhārata*'s narrative techniques.

Let us begin with the plot. Back in chapter two this story was summarized in only half a *śloka*: "The *Pauṣya* glorifies the greatness of Utanka"—but Utanka does not even appear until half-way through the chapter. Instead, the story begins with King Janamejaya being cursed because his brothers beat a dog. The dog's mother, "the bitch of the Gods," complains,

> "This son of mine did nothing wrong here! Why was he beaten? As he was beaten without doing wrong, therefore an unseen danger will befall you!" (44)

That is her curse. Distraught, Janamejaya (with his friend Pauṣya) goes in search of a priest who can help him. He finally chooses Somaśravas, the son of a hermit; but the hermit warns him,

> "Worthy Janamejaya, this son was born to me by a Snake woman.
>
> This great ascetic and accomplished student was begotten by the power of my austerities and grew in the womb of this Snake woman who had imbibed my seed.
>
> He is able to appease any evil deeds you may have done excepting the evil against the Great God.
>
> But he has sworn one secret vow—if a brahmin solicits any possession from him he must surrender it to him. If you will bear with that, take him with you!" (45)

Janamejaya accepts this condition, and goes off to conquer a city called Takṣaśilā. Except for the mention of Pauṣya, this little story has nothing at all to do with the rest of *Pauṣya*.

A long digression ensues, about a brahmin who has three students. This story will eventually weave its way back to Janamejaya, so perhaps it is not really a digression but a back-story preparing us for the next episode. In any case, this brahmin is severe with his students to the point of cruelty, submitting two of them to extreme tests of self-abnegation, austerity, and obedience. It is not clear what narrative purpose is served by the digressive stories of these two students; thematically, however, they certainly illustrate that cruelty is not just a kṣatriyan weakness. Brahmins can also be cruel. The third student, Veda, is spared these tests, but he too suffers, "like a bullock forever yoked to pull burdensome loads" (48).

Many years pass; now Veda has three students of his own, whom he does *not* test.

> He never told his students anything like "Observe this rite, obey your teacher";
> since he himself knew the sorrows of lodging at a teacher's house, he did not wish to burden his students with vexations. (48)

One of his students, however, Utanka (enter the hero at last), is tested by circumstances. While Veda is away, the women of the household urge Utanka to have sex with Veda's wife, and like the biblical Joseph, he refuses. On returning, Veda is so impressed that he considers Utanka's training complete, and dismisses him. But Utanka insists on giving him a guru gift, so Veda sends him to his wife to ask what gift she would like.

She requests a particular set of earrings from her husband's friend Pauṣya. Pauṣya, remember, is also Janamejaya's friend.

Getting the earrings turns out to be no easy task. On his quest for them Utanka has to solve a number of problems—one might say, pass a number of tests—all having to do with vows, curses, boons, obedience, and ritual purity. His quest also brings him into conflict with the King of the Snakes, Takṣaka, who, it turns out, also wants the earrings. Takṣaka is a trickster figure who will weave his way through many stories in the next fifty chapters. After Utanka finally acquires the earrings, Takṣaka steals them, and Utanka then has to go to the underworld to retrieve them. All of this happens in just a few pages.

In the end, Utanka succeeds in delivering the earrings to Veda's wife, but barely in time. Returning at the last possible moment, he narrowly avoids her curse. He is so outraged by this near-miss that he angrily swears vengeance on Takṣaka. Anger too is not just a kṣatriyan weakness, obviously. He hatches a plot to kill all the Snakes in the world—a bit of an over-reaction, to say the least. For this purpose he seeks out Janamejaya, to inform him that it was Takṣaka who killed his (Janamejaya's) father. Oddly, Janamejaya seems not to have known this fact.

So Utanka urges Janamejaya to perform the infamous Snake-Sacrifice. As the chapter closes, Janamejaya turns to his councilors and asks to hear the story of his father's death; but we will have to wait quite a while before we hear their reply—forty-three chapters, in fact. For all the action packed into every page, this story moves very, very slowly.

It is never made clear why the story should start with the dog, or why it should include all the stories of brahmins testing their students, or what connections there are, if any, between Janamejaya's choice of a priest, the circumstances of his father's death, and Utanka's quest, except that Snakes are somehow involved in all of them. We wait in vain for the curious detail of the young priest's vow—to surrender any possession to a brahmin who asks for it—to become a plot device. In fact, he immediately disappears from the poem (although in chapter five his father will reappear at the Snake Sacrifice). Also, we would like to know why the chapter is named for Pauṣya, who is such a minor character in the story. And why the forty-three chapter delay?

Mehta argues that the young priest's unfulfilled vow is a clue to the reason for the long delay; and both, it turns out, are clues to the history of the poem's composition. *Pauṣya* ends with Janamejaya's question to his councilors, but when we turn the page what do we find? Not the answer to his question; rather, with the next chapter, *Puloman*, the epic itself seems to start over—in fact, with the very same sentence as the first time. Once more the Bard arrives at the hermitage, but this time it is Śaunaka who greets him, not his hermits. This new beginning will lead, after fifty pages, to the same point at which we have already arrived. Mehta calls this "the problem of the double introduction":

> It leads with an identical beginning to the same situation of the narrative by a completely different path... It appears that we are in the presence of two different versions of the Janamejaya-sacrifice; one, older and in prose-form (Pauṣyaparvan) involving Uttanka and Somaśravas and some Brahmana (probably Āstīka) asking of Somaśravas to stop the sacrifice; and the other, more epic-like (Āstīka-parvan) involving Āstīka asking of Janamejaya to stop the sacrifice. (548-49)

And what about the curious detail of conquering Takṣaśilā? Does it have some connection to the Snake Takṣaka? Only at the very end of the *Mahābhārata* will we finally learn that Janamekaya's Snake Sacrifice was actually held at Takṣaśilā, a city noted in other sources for snakes and snake-worshipers (Minkowsky 391); it is not just a random detail, then—we just have to wait several thousand pages to see the point.

And what about the dog? We wait several thousand pages for that answer too, according to Hiltebeitel. In the final pages of the epic, the god Dharma comes to his son Yudiṣṭhira in the form of a dog, and Yudiṣṭhira's kindness to him turns out to be his penultimate test. Perhaps, Hiltebeitel suggests, the earlier episode was added at some point to balance the later one:

> Is the one dog story at the beginning of the epic left off to be picked up by the other at the end? Would Janamejaya's hearing it at the end have anything to do with his having abandoned the snake sacrifice at the beginning? (171)

The resulting paradox is a sort of karma in reverse: Janemajaya's crime at the beginning of the epic seems to be erased by Yudhiṣṭira's virtue at its conclusion, three generations earlier.

When we finally do hear the story of Janamejaya's father's death, we will be able to look back on *Pauṣya* and see that the only connection this chapter has to the larger story (not the main narrative, but just the frame story of the Snake Sacrifice) is that it poses for the first time the question, Why did Janamejaya want to destroy the Snakes? The reasons it offers are that Utanka was angered by a Snake, and Janamejaya's father was killed by a Snake. Forty-three chapters will go by before we actually hear that second story, about Janamajaya's father, and the intervening chapters will suggest much deeper reasons for the Snake Sacrifice anyway. What a roundabout way to tell a story!

Before moving on to the next chapter, let us read through this one again, more closely this time, because in our quick summary of it we have skipped over many of its episodes. For example, we compressed the account of Utanka's quest for the earrings into a single sentence, whereas in fact it fills four pages packed with fantastic details. Perhaps the deeper meaning of the chapter lies in that elaboration.

When Utanka refuses to be tempted by his teacher's wife, we can hardly avoid the comparison with Joseph, but the difference between the two is as surprising as the similarity. In gratitude for Utanka's virtue, Veda sends him to—of all people—his wife! "Go then and visit my wife, and ask her what you should bring. Bring whatever she demands." (49) Do we expect another temptation scene? She asks only for earrings. Then, when Utanka arrives at Pauṣya's court and requests the earrings, Pauṣya tells him, "Go to the women's quarters and ask the lady." (50) Another temptation scene? No, she is not there—or at least he cannot see her, because he is unclean. So he does his ablutions and returns to the women's quarters. Only then do we learn the real difficulty of his quest: Takṣaka wants the same earrings.

Utanka's four visits to the women's quarters are one structuring motif in the story, but there are others. Most notably, he has a series of puzzling supernatural adventures on his journey to and from Pauṣya's court, which Veda explicates to him afterwards. On his way there,

> he saw an oversized bull and, mounted on it, an oversized man. The man addressed Utanka: "Utanka, eat the dung of my bull!" He refused.
>
> Once more the man spoke: "Eat it, Utanka, do not hesitate. Your teacher himself has eaten it in his time."
>
> Hereupon Utanka said, "Surely!" and partook of the bull's dung and urine. (49-50)

On his return trip, when Takṣaka steals the earrings and dives into the underworld, Utanka hopes to draw him back by singing a song in praise of him and all the Snakes; when that trick does not work, Utanka sees a handsome man with an oversized horse, who saves the day:

> The man said to him "I am pleased with your song of praise. What favor can I do for you?"
>
> He said to him, "The Snakes shall be in my power!" The man replied, "Blow into this horse's arse."
>
> He blew the horse in the arse, whereupon from the blown-up horse smoking flames billowed out from all the orifices.
>
> With that he smoked out the world of the Snakes. Frenzied, desperately afraid of the hot power of the fire, Takṣaka seized the earrings, fled at once from his dwelling, and said to Utanka,
>
> "Sir, take back these earrings!" (52)

Why all this scatology? The first episode, with the dung and urine, would seem to account for Utanka's uncleanness when he arrives at the women's quarters. Afterwards, however, Veda explains to Utanka that the bull was really Airāvata, King of the Snakes (Takṣaka's brother, as we will learn in the *Epic of Āstīka*), and his dung and urine were actually the Elixir of Immortality (more about that in *Āstīka* too). Not only that, but the horse was actually the Fire God, Agni. Anyone who has blown into a fireplace to revive the flames will see the symbolism of blowing into the horse to make fire come out its orifices—and the humor of the image. These brahmins may be austere, but they are not humorless. In both of these episodes Utanka is presented with apparent conflicts between obedience and ritual purity. The teachings are counter-intuitive, ironic and amusing.

We have still skipped over several interesting episodes. These may at first strike us as trivial, but will seem less so when we read the next chapter. For example, before Utanka leaves Pauṣya's court, the two men suddenly fall into a cursing match. In general, the rule is that when words are uttered they cannot be retracted, and what is said must come to be. That will be a major plot device in the epic itself. But what if a curse is uttered hastily, in anger, or in error? The rules governing such cases are fairly refined.

Utanka, thinking he has intentionally been offered unclean food, impulsively curses Pauṣya with blindness; Pauṣya, outraged, impulsively curses Utanka in return with barrenness. When Pauṣya discovers that the food was indeed unclean, he apologizes; he then asks Utanka to withdraw his curse. Easier said than done, however: Utanka explains that a brahmin's curse cannot be withdrawn, although it can be modified; so he stipulates that Pauṣya's blindness be only temporary. And now it is Utanka's turn to ask Pauṣya to withdraw his curse. Again, easier said than done. Pauṣya explains that a kṣatriya's curse cannot be changed at all, for just as brahmins must be soft, kṣatriyas must be hard. Fortunately, our brilliant brahmin finds a loophole in all these rules: the wording of Pauṣya's curse assumed that the food was not unclean, but in fact it was; therefore he declares the curse invalid on technical grounds.

Succeeding chapters will focus more on just such subtleties of bramin-kṣatriya relations, not always in so amusing a form.

It is worth noting that thousands of pages later (XIV: 52-57) a variant version of the Utanka story will be told, different in many of its details, but also containing an impetuous curse, urine which is really the Elixir of Immortality, earrings stolen by a snake, and a horse smoking from all its orifices; and for those of us puzzled by the virtues of cow urine and dung, Bhīṣma in his death-bed sermon will explain why it is that the goddess Śrī inhabits the urine and dung of cows (XIII: 81). If we are patient enough, all of our questions will be answered.

7. *Puloman* (Chapters 4-12)

So now the poem begins again. Van Buitenen calls *Puloman* "the more formal opening" of the epic (xxii). The summary of *Puloman* back in chapter two simply says, "In *Puloman* the ramifications of the lineage of the Bhṛgus are described" (36).

Once more Ugraśravas arrives at Śaunaka's refuge; this time Śaunaka himself, rather than his hermits, comes out to greet him. He does not ask to hear the *Mahābhārata*, as they did in the first opening, but instead about his own ancestors, the Bhṛgus; so Ugraśravas's storytelling takes off in quite a different direction this time. As the first chapters told of Janamejaya's kṣatriyan ancestors, *Puloman* tells of Śaunaka's brahmin ancestors.

By Western literary standards, *Puloman* is a gem. It is divided into nine chapters, even though it is shorter than *Pauṣya*'s single one. It is also more unified, more charming, and more accessible in meaning than *Pauṣya*.

Ugraśravas tells two stories about Śaunaka's Bhṛgu ancestors. Each is neatly divided into two parts, a domestic tale and a theological lesson. A number of themes link the two stories, one of the most important being the one we just saw in *Pauṣya*, the subtle dynamics of curses. Being Bhṛgu stories, they also address the fundamental theme of the relations between brahmins and kṣatriyas.

The first story is about the birth of Śaunaka's great-great-great-grandfather, Cyavana, the son of Bhṛgu himself. Cyavana was dropped from his mother Pulomā's womb as she was being abducted, weeping, by a Rākṣasa (a forest demon) named Puloman. (The names Pulomā and Puloman are hopelessly confused in the Ganguli and Dutt translations.) Bhṛgu was out of the house at the time, doing his ablutions. It seems that Pulomā had once been betrothed to Puloman, but was given instead to Bhṛgu. That is Puloman's justification for the abduction. But before he abducts Pulomā, he calls on the sacrificial fire in the house (i.e., the god Agni) to testify to the broken betrothal. The fire does so, but only reluctantly; on the one hand, it must tell the truth, but on the other, it fears Bhṛgu's curse for doing so. It is at this point that Cyavana drops from his mother's womb. His brilliance immediately incinerates Puloman. In a lovely touch, Brahmā then turns Pulomā's tears into a river—which still flows, we are told, to Cyavana's hermitage.

Now Bhṛgu returns, and indeed he does curse Agni angrily. Suddenly the story of the abduction drops away, as if it had been only a pretext for introducing the problems that follow upon Bhṛgu's rash curse:

> In a rage he cursed the Fire, "Thou shalt eat anything!"
> But the Fire was outraged at the Bhṛgu's curse and said, "What new rashness hast thou wrought today, brahmin?
> "While I keep striving for the Law and speak the truth whatever comes, I was questioned and I spoke the truth.
> Where did I go wrong? I am no less capable of cursing you, but I must honor the brahmins...
> Through this mouth of mine are the ancestors given their offerings on new moon day, and the Gods on full moon day, and do they eat the offered oblation. How then should I, *their* mouth, become omnivorous?" (58-59)

The real issue is not the broken betrothal, it turns out, but ritual pollution. Only certain foods can be offered to the gods and the ancestors, and Bhṛgu's rash curse has inadvertently cancelled these rules. Outraged by Bhṛgu's curse, Agni withdraws from all sacrifices, precipitating a crisis for all brahmins. Brahmā then intervenes, negotiating the terms of sacrifice with Agni. He distinguishes between the fire within people, which burns food, and sacrificial fire, which is "the mouth of the gods and the ancestors." As a final safeguard, Brahmā finally proposes that "anything that has been burned by thy flames will be rendered pure" (59). Agni agrees, precisely in order to "make the seer's curse come true." How else to deal with a curse which is by definition effective, and which cannot be retracted? We will see in chapters to come that once a curse or prediction has been made, everyone is obliged to make it come true somehow, even when trying to obviate it. That often requires wit, and can be dangerous.

The discussion of ritual fire here gets surprisingly detailed; in fact, this episode is about as brahmanic as the *Mahābhārata* gets. Even those who talk of a thorough "brahmanization" of the epic admit that the many rituals in it (for example the two *sattras* of the frame) are almost never described in any detail (Minkowski 181; a rare counterexample is the story of Angiras in ch. 213 of Book III). In the end, this story about Śaunaka's Bhṛgu ancestor turns out to be an etiological tale explaining why ritual fire sanctifies anything placed in it as a sacrifice. Bhṛgu only enters the story briefly as a rash brahmin who nearly destroyed the brahmin world. What an odd way to satisfy Śaunaka's desire to hear stories of his ancestors.

It is worth noting, by the way, that this story does not involve Snakes. Bhṛgu must be important, to interrupt that theme. A story about the nature of ritual fire is always relevant at a *sattra*, but note that this story is not being told to Janamejaya at his *sarpa-sattra*.

The second story is about Śaunaka's great-grandfather Ruru. Ruru falls in love with the lovely nymph Pramadvarā, but before their wedding she is bitten by a snake and dies. Ruru is allowed by the gods to bring her back to life, by agreeing to give half of his own life-span to her (a Sleeping Beauty variant of the Innana, Persephone, Alcestis and Orpheus stories). She awakes, they marry, and his selfless love seems to be the point of this beautiful story.

However, from that day on, Ruru takes revenge on Snakes, killing every Snake he sees. Violence too is not just a kṣatriyan weakness, obviously. Note that all these stories are about brahmins who are in need of lessons. One day Ruru is about to strike a harmless Snake (perhaps not even a snake, but a lizard)—which turns out to be a brahmin (also, coincidentally, named Ruru), who at some time in the past was cursed by his teacher for frightening him with a snake made of grass (yet another case of a rash curse). The teacher impulsively cursed his playful student, and by its nature the curse could not be revoked, even though the teacher regretted it. As before, the only solution is to add a stipulation to the curse: in this case, the stipulation is that the curse will be lifted when in the distant future the student (now a Snake) meets our Ruru. Now that that has finally come to pass, the student is released from the curse, wiser for his experience.

It is as if the teacher had known that in the future another Ruru would need this particular wisdom, precisely at the moment when the curse is broken. The Snake Ruru now teaches our Ruru, who is obsessed with killing Snakes, the law of *ahiṃsā*—non-violence—which turns out to be the theological point of the story:

> "Non-injury is the highest Law known to all breathing creatures; therefore a brahmin gifted with breath shall nowhere kill any living creatures...
> Not to inflict hurt, to speak the truth, and to be forgiving is assuredly for the brahmin a Law even higher than preserving the Veda." (63)

Remember, this cycle of stories began with Janamejaya's brothers striking a dog for no purpose. Was that a violation of the rule of *ahiṃsā*? One might think so, but perhaps not. The rule of *ahiṃsā*, the Snake goes on to explain, only applies to brahmins, and Janamejaya, remember, is a kṣatryia.

> "The Law of the baron, however, that does not become you—to wield the staff, to be dreaded, and to protect the people.
> That was a baron's task—hear it from me, Ruru, who live by the Law—that hoary massacre of the Snakes by Janamejaya.
> And the salvation of the frightened Snakes was, at his Snake Sacrifice, to come from a brahmin alone, from Āstīka, foremost among the twice-born, O most excellent brahmin." (63)

That is, it is a kṣatriyan task to kill Snakes, and a brahmin task to save them. This will be a major theme in the next story, *Āstīka*.

Hiltebeitel says pregnantly, "The epic resists the universalization of ahiṃsā." (207) Few issues are more central to the *Mahābhārata* or more perplexing than this one, which we keep coming back to, the relation of brahmin wisdom to kṣatriyan rule, specifically of brahmin non-violence to kṣatriyan violence. Here we are approaching once more the vast overarching theme shared by the epic and its frame stories. Brahmin wisdom in the epic radiates non-violence, but the main narrative is about war, which has ethical laws of its own, and which would certainly seem to be violent. Brahmins are the highest class, charged with advising the other classes on issues of truth, wisdom and right behavior; so their ethic of non-violence stakes a claim to universality, even if the epic seems to resist it.

In the absence of other factors, *ahiṃsā* is a general law. But there *are* other factors, and they can be summed up in a word: *dharma*—i.e., laws specific to class, caste, gender, stage of life, etc. In general, it would seem, *dharma* trumps *ahiṃsā*. For kṣatriyas, whose *dharma* is to fight, that presents a contradiction, however, because *ahiṃsā* remains a universal law in other areas of life. In the *Bhagavad-Gītā* Kṛṣṇa preaches *ahiṃsā*, but at the same time urges Arjuna to fight. For the Western reader keen to resolve contradictions, that is as central and intractable a problem as the epic presents.

We have already encountered Biardeau's solution to the problem. According to her, the *Mahābhārata* proposes that the violence of war "cannot be called hiṃsā if this violence is not for the sake of killing but intended as sacrifice." (93) What that means, however, and whether it is the case, and, if it is, how it might apply to the Snake Sacrifice, we are still a long way from understanding; but at least now we know what question is being asked.

And now we can ask, What do these themes—wisdom and war, violence and non-violence—have to do with Śaunaka, to whom the story of Ruru is being told? The Snake's speech has an especial force in this Bhṛgu setting, for Bhṛgus, remember, are brahmins who act like kṣatriyas. The teaching of *ahiṃsā* would seem to undermine Bhṛgu ideology. Śaunaka, who is a Bhṛgu, is being told by the Bard that brahmins must not indulge in violence—not even the killing of Snakes. Hiltebeitel says,

> Having learned that the only way to bring his snake-bitten fiancée back to life is to give her half the lifetime still ahead of him, Ruru does this, but then goes around clubbing snakes to death until he learns from a lizard, whom he is ready to kill as a snake, that he is acting more like a Kṣatriya, and in particular like Janamejaya, than a *Brahmān*. (113)

The point of the frame story of the Snake Sacrifice is slowly coming clearer: in holding such a sacrifice, Janamejaya is following the law of the kṣatriya; in preventing it, Āstīka is following the law of the brahmin. The story of the sacrifice, with its two intertwined plots, is therefore a parable of relations between the two classes, filled with contradiction and conflict, but neatly balanced. We find hints of this balance in all these amusing stories about curses, but only in the story of the Snake Sacrifice itself, the story of Āstīka, will the conflicting claims of the two classes in the *Mahābhārata* be resolved.

There is something else to note before we put *Puloman* aside. It is easy to overlook the biggest surprise of all in the story's conclusion. The Snake offers Āstīka's rescue of the Snakes at Janamejaya's sacrifice as an object lesson in brahmin *ahiṃsā*: "the salvation of the frightened Snakes was, at his Snake Sacrifice, to come from a brahmin alone." The Snake tells Ruru that he is acting, as Hiltebeitel paraphrases it, "more like Janamejaya than a Brahman." But Janamejaya's Snake Sacrifice has not yet happened. Ruru lived three generations before Janamejaya. Is this flagrant violation of chronology a mistake? Is Vyāsa nodding? Again, one might think so, but again, probably not. In the long story of Āstīka there will be several of these Escher-like Moebius loops in the narrative. We must learn to accept them as a stylistic (or philosophical, or cultural) feature of the *Mahābhārata*.

As *Puloman* ends, Ruru rushes home to his father, to learn from him the story of Āstīka. Both *Pauṣya* and *Puloman* end with someone asking for the next story. If that reminds us of the *1001 Nights*, that is probably because the author of the *1001 Nights* learned it from the *Mahābhārata*.

8. *Āstīka* (Chapters 13-24)

Predictably, we do not hear the story of Āstīka from Ruru's father. How could he have known it anyway, since he lived several generations before it took place? Then again, such time-bending is common in the *Mahābhārata*. Out in the outer frame, however, Śaunaka wants to hear the story, so the Bard proceeds to recount to him the rescue of the Snakes, first in summary, and then at enormous length. The rationale for this huge account (half again as long as everything we have read so far) is to answer Śaunaka's opening questions:

> "Why did King Janamejaya, a tiger among kings, carry on with the full Snake Sacrifice until all Snakes were finished? Tell me that!
> And why did that excellent brahmin Āstīka, the best of the mumblers of spells, have the Snakes set free from the fire that had blazed forth?
> Whose son was that king who offered the Snake Sacrifice? And tell me, whose son was that eminent brahmin?" (68-69)

He wants both stories, the one about the king's motivation and the one about the brahmin's, and he wants their parents' stories too—all of which will eventually intersect at the story's climax.

As the *Iliad* asks "what happened?" the *Mahābhārata* asks "why did it happen?"—in this case, why did Janamejaya and Āstīka act as they did? Simplifying somewhat, we might say that whereas the *Iliad* explores the consequences of an action, the *Mahābhārata* explores the causes of one. Why do things happen? There are causes for any event, usually many causes, related or unrelated, and those causes have causes too. In the *Mahābhārata* there are so many causes that if the rationale for telling the story is to answer the question Why, then many, many stories will need to be told. The narrative plunges farther and farther back into the past, ranging from back-story to back-story, weaving them all together, all of them contributing to the same eventual outcome, but challenging us along the way to comprehend their spider-webbing structures. The more causes adduced, of course, the more inevitable—fated—their end will seem. That is not exactly to say that something called Fate causes things to happen, however, since many of the causes do involve human agency. There is always room for moral action. The issue is complex, to say the least.

In school I learned that it was a joke to ask the causes of the First World War, because there were so many. That would not stop the authors of the *Mahābhārata*! In this respect, the nearest Western analogue to the epic's narrative technique is not the *Iliad*, but *War and Peace*. In that novel Tolstoy explores the causes of the War of 1812, as Vyāsa explores the causes of the Bhārata war (well, after the Bard first explores the causes of the Snake Sacrifice at which Vyāsa's account of the war was recited). What Tolstoy says about causes in general applies perfectly in both of these cases:

> To us, their descendants, ... an incalculable number of causes present themselves. The deeper we delve in search of these causes the more of them we find; and each separate cause or whole series of causes appears to us equally valid in itself... Without each of these causes nothing could have happened. So all these causes—myriads of causes—coincided to bring it about. So there was no one cause for that occurrence, but it had to occur

> because it had to... A deed done is irrevocable, and its result coinciding in time with the actions of millions of other men assumes an historic significance... When an apple has ripened and falls, why does it fall? Because of its attraction to the earth, because its stalk withers, because it is dried by the sun, because it grows heavier, because the wind shakes it, or because the boy standing below wants to eat it? (537-38)

Tolstoy's approach to narrative and history in *War and Peace* is unique in Western literature, but readers of Indian literature might find it oddly familiar. They might call it *karmic narrative*, in which history is too complex and organic to be analyzed fully; in which even the smallest actions have enormous consequences; and in which things happen, in large part, because they must.

Even considering all of Śaunaka's questions, however, only a tiny portion of the *Epic of Āstīka* will seem even remotely relevant to them, at least at first. The summary of it back in chapter two simply said, "In Āstīka the birth of Garuḍa and all the Snakes, the churning of the milky sea, and the origin of Uccaiḥśravas." Those three stories all concern Snakes in one way or another, but what do they have to do with the Snake-seer Āstīka? The *Epic of Āstīka* looks like a highly baroque and dazzling elaboration of mythology, seemingly for its own sake. The only way a first reader can approach it, of course, is chapter by chapter, so that is what we will do, from chapter thirteen all the way to chapter fifty-six.

Ch. 13. First the Bard (Sauti) gives a summary of the story, only two pages long. He relates the birth of "the most glorious Āstīka," who is obviously going to be the hero of the story. Āstīka's father and mother were both named Jaratkāru, and each of them has a back-story. The father Jaratkāru was a brahmin ascetic. In his wanderings he stumbled upon his ancestors hanging like bats in a cave. They told him that if he did not have a son, their line would go extinct. Their plea might at first sight seem startling in the brahmin context, because we might hold an inaccurate stereotype of brahmins as celibate ascetics.

> "By neither merits of Law nor high-piled austerities do people in this world gain the goal that others reach by having sons.
> Put your efforts into wedding a wife, and your mind on begetting offspring, as we now instruct you, son of ours!" (69)

Ascetic life may be good, but life itself depends upon marriage and procreation. If the *Mahābhārata* is brahmin propaganda, it is obviously propaganda aimed at brahmins as much as kṣatriyas, and contains a good deal of brahmin self-criticism. Brahmins should not act like kṣatriyas, but the opposite extreme, "high-piled austerities," seems also to be a danger.

The issue being raised here is the relationship between brahmin life as it is defined in the Vedas, and the ascetic/hermit life which evolved as an alternative to it during the period represented in the Upanishads. Brahmin life in the earlier period revolved around the performance of rituals, especially sacrifices. Brahmin life as it is described in the Upanishads, on the other hand, is anti-ritualistic; sacrificial rites have been replaced by acts of renunciation and self-mortification. One does not sacrifice animals any more, one sacrifices one's self. It is commonly said that in the Upanishads the old Vedic rituals have been *interiorized*. Remember what the Snake told Ruru only a few pages ago:

> "Not to inflict hurt, to speak the truth, and to be forgiving is assuredly for a brahmin a Law even higher than preserving the Veda." (63)

Jaratkāru's ancestors, however, are here articulating the older, more traditional point of view. They are obviously anticelibate, anti-renunciatory, and ritualistic. That seems to be the point.

It would be too simple to say that brahminism simply changed from one form to another, from ritual to renunciation, or that these two forms were mutually exclusive. In the *Mahābhārata*, at least, they co-exist, however awkwardly. Armstrong says, "Even though the later literature would present the renouncer as the ideal Brahmin, and tried to incorporate him into Vedic orthodoxy, in fact he challenged the entire system." (124) The "later literature" she is referring here to includes the *Mahābhārata*, which tries to meet that challenge by incorporating the newer forms of renunciation into the older brahmin ritualism. One way of doing that is to theorize them as two kinds of sacrifice. The results are sometimes awkward. According to Sullivan, for example, Vyāsa "both embodies the ancient traditions of Vedic Brahminism and certain of the newer traditions which were finding their place in emergent Hinduism." (27) It is a balancing act.

Jaratkāru, in his own balancing act in this episode, reluctantly agrees to marry in order to save his ancestors, but places three seemingly impossible restrictions on his promise: (1) he will only marry a woman with his own name; (2) she must be cffered to him of her own free will, as alms; and (3) he must not be expected to maintain her. Exactly why he insists on these conditions is left unexplained.

It is not enough for van Buitenen to point out "the well-known motif of the three impossible conditions, which are yet miraculously met" (444). The reader wants to know why, if Jaratkāru really wants to save his ancestors, he imposes these seemingly impossible conditions. Is this the poet's way of representing ambivalence toward marriage? Jaratkāru does not seem very ambivalent in his search:

> Henceforth this brahmin of strict vows roamed the earth, searching for a wife to set up house, but he did not find her.
>
> One day the brahmin went into the forest and, calling to mind the words of his forebears and longing for a maiden who was to be given him as an alms, he softly wept his three words. (70)

Perhaps the story is etiological: perhaps the conditions—at least two of them—are being offered as normative marriage customs. Brahmin ascetics are expected to marry, we are being taught, but they cannot be expected to pay bride-gifts, or support their families.

When Jaratkāru finally does marry, the Bard summarizes his brahmin duties this way:

> With manifold vows and Vedic studies, O brahmin, he acquitted himself of his debts: the Gods he satisfied with sacrifices of various stipends, the seers with his scholarship, and his ancestors with progeny. (71)

That is, a brahmin is expected to perform the rituals as a means of support, to study, and to have a family—what is sometimes called "the theology of the three debts." It is the old way, here laying claim to a renunciate of the new way. Like Vyāsa, Jaratkāru somehow embodies both Vedic ritualism and renunciate anti-ritualism at the same time.

When Jaratkāru softly weeps his three words in the forest, the miracle happens. A woman named Jaratkāru is suddenly offered to him willingly as alms by her brother, the Snake Vāsuki (yet another of Takṣaka's brothers). How this coincidence could have happened—how Vāsuki knew of Jaratkāru's vow to marry only someone of the same name, eons before that vow was made, and how he guarded his sister from birth so that she could eventually fulfill that vow, and his motive for offering her—all that will turn out to be the heart of *The Epic of Āstīka*. Here in the Bard's opening summary, however, that enormous back-story-to-come is referred to only fleetingly:

> The Snakes had once been cursed by their mother: "Fire who is driven by Wind shall burn you at Jamamejaya's sacrifice."
> It was to appease this curse that the princely Snake gave his sister to the great-spirited seer of good vows. (70)

Ch. 14. After hearing this provocative summary—a narrative so mysteriously improbable that one simply needs to know more—Śaunaka asks to hear the full version. So the Bard starts all over again, this time beginning, "Long ago, in the Eon of the Gods... " (71)

We have already learned the immediate cause of the Snake Sacrifice: Utanka told Janamejaya that Janamejaya's father was killed by the Snake Takṣaka, so he should kill all Snakes. That, however, was only the *immediate* cause (only one of three immediate causes which Janamejaya will eventually itemize). There was also an *ultimate* cause, and that is the curse laid on all Snakes by their mythical mother Kadrū, shortly after the Creation. There is also an ultimate cause for Āstīka's interruption of the sacrifice, and that cause is Vāsuki's plot to undo Kadrū's curse, in order to save himself and his fellow Snakes.

It will take twenty-five pages to tell just this primeval part of the story. It is a narrative of stunning complexity, which requires close attention. It begins with "the birth of Garuḍa and all the Snakes, the churning of the milky sea, and the origin of Uccaiḥśravas." Only after those stories are told will we return to the two Jaratkārus, the birth of Āstīka, and, finally the Snake Sacrifice itself, where the Bard first heard Vaiśaṃpāyana recite the *Mahābhārata*; and only then will we ourselves finally be able to read the *Mahābhārata* that he heard. (Of course we are already reading the *Mahābhārata*, but a later one, which includes this story of its own telling.)

It is almost impossible to summarize this part of the poem. Perhaps that is why the Bard did not even attempt it in his initial summary. Here the narrative suddenly explodes into the fully irrational chaos of uninhibited mythology, with dozens of overlapping, intersecting, layered, contradictory and unchronological back-stories, a jumble of motifs and narrative threads that can hardly be disentangled, stretching over twenty-two chapters. It is extremely impressive, as myth always is when unmediated by analysis. One thinks of the Mesopotamian *Enuma Elish*, Hesiod's *Theogony*, Ovid's *Metamorphoses* and the Norse *Edda*. We could, if we like, recast the story into a more linear form for clarity, but that would only convert an ancient Indian way of telling the story to a modern Western way. Rather, our experience of reading the narrative needs to take the following confusing form.

The story begins. Angry at her Snake-children for not being eager to help her in a dispute with her sister and co-wife Vinatā, Kadrū condemns them to be burned at some time in the distant future in a sacrifice by King Janamejaya. Thus Janamejaya's sacrifice has been pre-destined, or at least predicted, virtually from the beginning of the world, "in the Eon of the Gods." Hearing this, Śaunaka wants to know what the dispute between the sisters was which brought about the curse. Well, the Bard explains, they were arguing about the color of the horse Uccaiḥśravas, who was born when the Gods churned the ocean to create the Elixir of Immortality. And what is that story? Śaunaka asks. Thus the narrative proceeds backwards, branching into more and more causes.

In chapter fourteen the poets begin by explaining that Kadrū and Vinatā were the co-wives of the brahmin Kaśyapa. Like Bhṛgu, Kaśyapa is the founder of a brahmin clan, and as one of the "Seven Sages" he is also the incarnation of a demiurge present at the world's creation. This part of the story involves the celestial Kaśyapa, though he is sometimes also depicted in his brahmin human form. These are a little hard to distinguish. Myth is inherently confusing to someone trying to "straighten it out."

In any case, Kaśyapa gave his two wives boons. Kadrū chose as her boon to have a thousand Snakes as offspring; Vinatā chose to have just two offspring, both birds, both of them better than Snakes. So Kadrū bore a thousand eggs, and Vinatā two. Birds and Snakes are obviously related, both being egg-layers; like brahmins, they are *dvija*, "twice-born." After only five hundred years, Vinatā impatiently opened her first egg—with the result that her first child, Aruṇa (Dawn), was born deformed. For this impatience, Aruṇa cursed his mother to be the slave of her sister Kadrū for five hundred years—adding that if only she will care for her second egg properly, for at least five hundred more years, her second son will end her slavery. (Do these numbers make sense? Would her curse not be over by the time the second egg hatched?) This time she is patient, and five hundred years later Garuḍa (King of the Birds, commonly identified with the

Sun) is born, and he immediately flies away. His story will be told in due time.

Chs. 15-17. Now the two sisters see the horse—but of course Śaunaka interrupts:

> "How did the gods churn for the Elixir, and tell me, where? And where was that mighty and resplendent prince of horses born?" (72)

So the Bard happily digresses for three chapters. The Gods, he says, wishing for the Elixir of Immortality, asked the Snake Ananta (yet another of Takṣaka's brothers) to uproot a mountain to use as a churning staff, and used Vāsuki as a churning rope. The result is well worth quoting at length:

> from the churning ocean there arose the Sun of a hundred thousand rays, which seemed to equal it, and the bright cool Moon of the tranquil light.
>
> And Goddess Śrī came forth from the butter, clothed in white robes, and the Goddess Liquor, and the White Horse;
>
> and the divine and lustrous Kaustubha jewel that hangs on Nārāyaṇa's chest, resplendent in its radiance, rose from the Elixir.
>
> Śrī, Liquor, the Moon, and the Horse swift as thought all followed the path of the Sun to where the Gods were standing.
>
> And now came forth the beautiful God Dhanvantari who carried a white gourd that held the Elixir.
>
> When they saw this great marvel, a loud outcry for the Elixir went up from the Dānavas, who screeched, "It is mine!"

> But Lord Nārāyaṇa employed his bewitching wizardry and assumed the wondrous shape of a woman: then he joined the Dānavas.
> Their minds bewitched, they gave that woman the Elixir, both Dānavas and Daityas did, for their hearts went out to her. (74)

The Gods drink the Elixir, but immediately the demons (Daityas and Dānavas) attack to capture it for themselves. Viṣṇu (Nārāyaṇa) throws off his "incomparably beautiful body of a woman" (75), and there ensues a terrific war in heaven, extremely violent and chaotic. The two armies end up throwing mountains at each other. Eventually the Gods win. Anyone familiar with Mesopotamian, Greek and Germanic mythology, or even *Paradise Lost*, will find numerous analogues here. The divine battle between the gods and demons will be one of many parallels and motives offered in the poem for the historical battle between the Pāṇḍavas and Kauravas.

What about the Elixir? It grants immortality to anyone who drinks it. It is the exclusive property of the gods, and the explanation of their immortality, but as in many mythologies (for example, the *Epic of Gilgamesh*), snakes have a special claim on it because snakes shed their skins, an obvious and widespread symbol of rejuvenation or rebirth. In the course of our story the Elixir will be revealed also to be Soma, the brahmin ritual drink. The churning of the ocean, then, is at one level a representation of the procedure for making Soma, in a churn of some sort, with milk, a churning stick and a rope. The narrative is very overdetermined; it means any number of things at once.

Chs. 18-19. Enough of that back-story for the moment. Now back to the sisters, who finally set their wager on the color of the horse. The horse Uccaiḥśravas is legendarily white (like milk, like the ocean's foam), so what is there to wager about? Kadrū tells her Snake-children to insert themselves into the horse's tail for a touch of black; but they hesitate to help her cheat in this way, so she curses them to be destroyed someday in the distant future, in Janamejaya's sacrifice. Not liking Snakes, the Gods approve of her curse; but Brahmā thinks it too severe, there being good Snakes as well as bad—after all, Ananta and Vāsuki just helped churn the ocean—so he modifies the curse by giving Kaśyapa the power to heal snake poisoning. That is not exactly logical, it is not exactly a modification of the curse, but it makes a certain kind of sense, and it will return as a plot device later.

The sisters wait for dawn to see the horse again. In the morning they view the ocean, a terrifying vision of chaos. Just looking at the ocean is enough to explain where the myth of its churning comes from. Chapter nineteen's description of the ocean is a majestic set-piece worth quoting at length, but a few verses will have to do:

> Terror of the creatures, ever-restless holder of the waters, resplendent and divine spring of the Immortals' Elixir, beyond measure and imagining, most sacred and marvelous,
> it is also dreadful and gruesome with the screechings of its denizens and its fearsome reverberations, aswirl with abysmal maelstroms and a danger to all beings.
> Stirring with the winds and the shifting of its tidelines, then rising up with quakes and turbulence, it seems to dance all about to the rhythm of its rippling hands,
> its waves imperviously swelling with the waxing and the waning of the moon. (77)

Chs. 20-24. With the help of the Snakes, Kadrū wins the wager, resulting in Vinatā's being enslaved to her. *What?* Obviously the Snakes changed their minds about helping their mother, but their change of mind is not mentioned in the Critical Edition. Van Buitenen throws up his hands at the "flagrant contradiction," noting dismissively that the Vulgate repairs it. (443) In any case, we now have two explanations of how Vinatā became her sister's slave: Aruṇa's curse, and losing the wager. Perhaps different versions of the same story have been melded together over time. Perhaps the "double introduction" of the *Mahābhārata* is like the two accounts of Creation in *Genesis*, and doublets like Vinatā's double curse and the two versions of the Utanka story are like the two interwoven stories of the Noah's Ark. However, so little effort has gone into disguising such contradictions that perhaps it is more than just a problem for textual analysis and source-study. Perhaps in Indian narrative, events and actions really *can* have multiple causes; or perhaps it is just that myth, unlike history, does not disallow differing versions of a narrative.

At this point the poet launches into another digression—if anything in such a wandering narrative as this one has become can be called a digression—fully eleven chapters long. It is the story of how Garuḍa stole the Elixir.

> Garuḍa when his time had come broke the shell of his egg
> and was born in all his might without help from his mother.
> Ablaze like a kindled mass of fire, of most terrifying aspect,
> the Bird grew instantly to his giant size and took to the sky.

> Upon seeing him all the Gods took refuge with the bright-shining Bird; and prostrating themselves they spoke to him of the many hues as he sat perched:
> "Fire, deign to grow no more! Would that thou do not seek to burn us." (78)

Garuḍa goes to see his mother, who has been reduced to slavery. Finding himself doing the Snakes' bidding and not knowing why, he asks her for an explanation. When she explains how she was cheated, he asks the Snakes,

> "What can I fetch you or find you, or what feat can I perform so that I may be freed from being bound to you? Speak the truth, Snakes!"
> The Snakes answered: "Bring us the Elixir with all your might, then you shall be freed from your slavery!" (80-81)

So he sets out to steal the Elixir of Immortality. It is a complicated narrative of several episodes, all quite hallucinatory, with an amusing trick ending: Garuḍa will fetch the Elixir, but the Snakes will never get to drink it—snakes may shed their skins, but they are not really immortal, after all.

We cannot help but think of this as the Garuḍa story, but it is also part of the Elixir of Immortality story, which started back in chapter thirteen with the birth of the horse Uccaiḥśravas in the Churning of the Ocean story, which are all parts of the Snake Sacrifice frame story. Since this is a lot to keep in mind, and since the narrative is about to take another quite surprising turn, we might take a moment to consider how we got here.

9. Taking Stock

When we first opened the *Mahābhārata*, we found ourselves at a performance of the epic by a wandering bard at a hermitage in the Naimiṣa forest. The Bard began by explaining to his audience of monks how he came to know the *Mahābhārata*. He said he heard it first at Janamejaya's Snake Sacrifice. The monks asked him to tell them about that first, so he put off telling the *Mahābhārata* to tell them how Janamejaya convened his great Snake Sacrifice. He convened it because (1) he was avenging his father, who was killed by the Snake Takṣaka (we still have not heard that story), and also because (2) he was fulfilling (unknowingly) a curse made on Snakes by their mother at the beginning of the world. The monks then asked to hear the story of that curse, so the Bard put off the story of the Snake Sacrifice to tell them about the birth of the Snakes and Birds from the two sisters, Kaśyapa's wives, and how the curse on Snakes that led to Janamejaya's sacrifice was the result of their wager over the color of the horse that was born when the gods churned the ocean to make the Elixir of Immortality. Of course the monks then asked to hear about that, so the Bard put off telling them about the curse on Snakes, which would have led us back to Janamejaya's sacrifice, and launched instead into the story of the Elixir. After several chapters, that story has now converged with the story of the two sisters, in the story of how Garuḍa stole the Elixir from the gods. What any of this has to do with the *Mahābhārata* itself is anybody's guess. We are mighty far from that story, and about to go several steps farther.

Every time the Bard breaks off one story to tell another, however, we can rest assured that he will eventually get back to it. This is the "embedding" technique that Minkowski says is typical of the brahmin rituals that are the poem's frame settings. His description of the technique makes it sound a little neater than it is in practice, however, for it is often difficult to tell where an embedded story begins and where it ends, and besides, it may be told twice or more, in different forms, quite far apart.

We are about to come to another of these embedded stories. Just as we discovered that behind the story of Janamejaya's revenge for his father's death there was a mythical story driving it, i.e., Kadrū's curse on Snakes, we are about to discover that there is yet another level of narrative driving that myth in turn; for Garuḍa's theft of the Elixir will turn out to have been pre-destined by an even earlier back-story, concerning Kaśyapa and the brahmins of the forest. It is in this layer of the story that the Elixir is equated most explicitly with Soma. We seem to be in the middle of an etiological tale of how brahmins came to possess their divine ritual drink, a tale strongly reminiscent (or *pre*miniscent, rather) of the Norse myth of how Thor stole back the mead which is the divine drink of poetry, told in the *Eddas*.

Notice that in these chapters all the focus is on brahmins rather than kṣatriyas. For example, as Garuḍa sets out to steal the Elixir in order to free his mother Vinatā from her slavery to her sister, she instructs him never to harm brahmins:

> "On a solitary ocean bay lies the great realm of those thousands of Niṣādas. Have your meal of those thousands of Niṣādas and bring the Elixir.
>
> But never set your mind on killing a brahmin. Among all creatures the brahmin, like fire, should never be killed.

> A brahmin angered is a fire, a sun, a poison, a sword. The brahmin is the first eater among all beings, the first among all classes, the father, the techer." (81)

We are deep inside the brahmin part of the *Mahābhārata*, the mythicized part, which van Buitenen finds so inept, silly and foolish.

10. Back to Garuḍa
(*Āstīka*, Chapters 24-30)

His mother's advice about brahmins in mind, Garuḍa flies up into the sky. He soon discovers, however, that he cannot get his fill of Niṣādas without scooping up brahmins with them. Niṣādas are outcastes of mixed brahmin-śūdra parentage, typically described as fishermen or hunters. They are not very filling anyway, so what will Garuḍa eat on his way to get the Soma? Suddenly his father Kaśyapa appears with a solution: he knows an elephant and a tortoise who should be eaten. But first, of course, he has to tell the story of why the elephant and the tortoise are enemies, and why they deserve to be killed. They are actually two brahmin brothers who wickedly cursed each other into their present forms.

So Garuḍa grabs the elephant and the tortoise in his claws, and flies to a great tree where he can eat them; but the branch breaks beneath his weight, and when he grabs the branch in his beak he notices, with a smile, that a clan of tiny brahmins called the Vālakhilyas are hanging upside-down from it like bats. Now he cannot drop the branch for fear of killing the brahmins. At which point he sees his father Kaśyapa on a mountaintop, "standing in self-mortification." It is worth quoting a few lines here, just to sample the extreme style that the narrative has arrived at in its rapid surreal development:

> And the father saw the divinely colored Bird,
> filled with glow, might and strength, swift as mind and wind, huge like a mountain peak, who rose like the upraised staff of Brahmā—

beyond imagining and comprehension, terror of all creatures, wielder of the power of wizardry, the upthrusting kindled fire incarnate—

unassailable and invincible to Gods, Dānavas and Rākṣasas, cleaver of mountaintops, drier of the water of the rivers,

whirler of the worlds, awesome image of Death. Seeing him come and surmising his intentions, the blessed Kaśyapa said the words:

"Son, do not act rashly, lest you incur sudden pain, lest the sunbeam-drinking Vālakhilyas wax angry and burn you!"

Thereupon, for his son's sake, Kaśyapa appeased the Vālakhilyas of accomplished austerities, pointing out the purpose of it:

"The good of the creatures is served by Garuḍa's enterprise, ye ascetics. He seeks to do a great feat; pray give him your leave!"

At these words of the blessed Kaśyapa the sages left the branch and together they repaired to the holy Mount Himālaya, in search of austerities.

When they had departed, Vinatā's son, his beak still distended by the branch, asked his father Kaśyapa,

"Sir, where can I let go of this tree limb? Is there a country without brahmins?" (84)

When Garuḍa finally drops the branch on a remote mountain (and finally eats the elephant and tortoise), the Gods are so frightened by the noise that they begin attacking each other in an even greater war than before, complete with meteors and showers of blood. When Indra asks the meaning of these portents, he is told,

> "It is through your own fault, Lord of the Gods, and your own negligence, you of the hundred sacrifices, that the Vālakhilyas have armed themselves with the power of their austerities and engendered a marvelous creature.
> It is a Bird, son of Kaśyapa the sage and Vinatā, powerful and of many disguises; and he has now come to steal the Soma." (85)

Now this is news: how is Garuḍa's attack *Indra's* fault? And how was Garuḍa engendered by the *Vālakhilyas*? Śaunaka, naturally, interrupts to ask for explanations of these surprising revelations:

> "How had the great Indra been at fault, and where had he been negligent, son of the Bard?
> And how indeed did Kaśyapa, who was a brahmin, beget a son who became King of the Birds through the austerities of the Vālakhilyas?" (86)

Now the Bard provides the final back-story to all these back-stories.

When the brahmin Kaśyapa wished to beget a son, he explains, he offered a sacrifice, and forced both Indra and the Vālakhilyas to gather firewood for it. The tiny Vālakhilyas found themselves being mocked for their size by the giant Indra; they retaliated by vowing that Kaśyapa's son would be born "a second Indra":

> "There shall be another Indra to all the Gods, with every power at his call, and with every range at his will, who shall be the terror of Indra," they announced, strict in their vows.

> "As the fruit of our austerities there shall now arise a terrible creature, swift as thought, who shall match Indra a hundredfold in power and bravery!" (86)

Indra, terrified by their curse, consulted Kaśyapa. As usual, the curse could not be withdrawn, only modified. Kaśyapa, not wanting to anger Indra, negotiated a solution. He asked the Vālakhilyas to modify the vow so that the second Indra would only be an Indra *of the birds* (a way of saying "lord of the birds"). Out of respect, they agreed. That accomplished, Kaśyapa announced to Vinatā,

> "You shall give birth to two heroic sons, overlords of the three worlds, who will be born from the austerities of the Vālakhilyas and from my own intention" (87).

And that is how the Vālakhilyas brought it about that Garuḍa was born to be a new Indra. Kaśyapa then addressed Indra:

> "Nevermore hold light these scholars of the Brahman, nor ever pridefully despise them: their wrath is fierce, their word is poison." (87)

So the gods walk in fear of brahmins!

But how can it be, Western readers might ask, that this narrative behind the myth is set back in the world of brahmins, as if that world—our world—were ontologically prior? We are reminded of a similar paradox in the *Iliad*: the reason Poseidon hates Troy is that the Trojan king Leomedon hired him to build the city walls, and then refused to pay him. Are human beings, then, superior to the gods, that they can hire them and cheat them?

The Greek analogy does not make the Indian case any easier to understand. From a Western point of view it remains shocking that Indian religion privileges the brahmin not only socially but ontologically. It is assumed (in brahmin writings, of course) that the stability and continuity of the universe depends upon brahmin prayer, ritual, sacrifice, austerities, meditation, and other spiritual practices. That is what explains the creative power of brahmin curses, vows and predictions: brahmins possess divine power. In chapter sixty we will learn that the brahmin Bhṛghu was born directly from Brahmā's heart; likewise Kaśyapa is Brahmā's own grandson. Even more surprising,

> "From Kaśyapa were born the Gods and Asuras, O tiger among kings—he is the origin of the worlds." (149)

Not only are the gods at the brahmin's beck and call, therefore, but the gods' powers and their very existence depend upon brahmin austerities—*tapas* (literally "heat"). Van Buitenen explains this key term:

> While it surely has connections with the heat of priests at fire sacrifices, the term comes to describe any specific act of self-deprivation aimed at an increase in spiritual power... The power thus acquired makes the ascetics a kind of new Gods on earth, rivaling and surpassing the Gods, and divinely unpredictable. While in Buddhism and Jainism such self-mortification is directed toward release from transmigration, this is distinctly understated in the *Mahābhārata*. The ascetics are bent on their own purposes. (436)

The *Mahābhārata*, that is, presents an extreme case of the humanist's paradox: the gods did not create men; rather, men created the gods. This simple formula does not quite fit the Indian situation, however, because in India there is not such a clear-cut distinction between gods and men to begin with.

To make matters even odder for a Western reader, the divinity of those brahmins who created the gods cannot be relied upon to serve the interests of mankind, any more than the gods themselves can be. In the *Mahābhārata*, some of those capable of achieving divinity by means of austerities are totally self-interested, or even evil. Even demons are capable of defeating the gods by means of great austerities. In the case we are coming to, for example, brahmins can threaten and command even Indra himself. As odd as that may sound to Western readers of Homer, it is by no means unusual in the Indian context. Indra, after all, is only a warrior god, whereas brahmins are descended from Brahmā; and brahmins are superior to kṣatriyas.

Now let us return to the story of Garuḍa: he invades heaven, scatters the Gods, gathers up the Soma, and defeats Indra with a single feather. Impressed, Indra offers him his friendship and a boon. Garuḍa accepts, but with one condition:

> "I am the master of all, but still I shall become your suppliant: let the mighty Snakes become my staple, Indra!" (90)

Now we know why birds eat snakes. Then, finally, Garuḍa returns to trick the Snakes into freeing his mother from slavery. When he delivers the Soma, thus fulfilling their demand, he reminds them to purify themselves with a bath before drinking it, and as they do so, Indra steals it back.

11. Back to the Snakes
(*Āstīka*, Chapters 31-46)

All this, and we are only half-way through *Āstīka*. But at least we are finally back at the story of Kadrū's curse on the Snakes: for Śaunaka now asks how the Snakes responded to being cursed by their mother to die at Janamejaya's sacrifice.

The narrative has been confusing enough so far, but the rest of Āstīka is among the most involuted and disorienting narratives one is ever likely to encounter. We will often find ourselves asking, "Who's on first?"

Chs. 31-32. What do the Snakes do when their mother Kadrū curses them? Her first son, Śeṣa, retires to the mountains to perform austerities. When Brahmā asks why, Śeṣa explains that he is disgusted by his brothers' hatred of Garuḍa. After all, Garuḍa is their brother too. For this excellent answer Brahmā offers him a boon. Śeṣa requests only that he might rejoice in the Law. Doubly impressed, Brahmā decrees that the whole earth shall be made steady in Śeṣa's embrace, and he turns him into Ananta, the serpent who holds up the earth, and he makes Garuḍa Ananta's helper.

But wait: there is a serious contradiction here. Was it not Ananta who uprooted the mountain for the Gods when they needed to churn the ocean, and was that not *before* the horse was created, and therefore before Kadrū's curse was pronounced? Śeṣa could not have been turned into Ananta *after* the curse, if Ananta already existed *before* the curse. The contradiction is quite obvious—more obvious than some others we have noticed, like the Snake telling Ruru that he is behaving like Janamejaya at the Snake Sacrifice, three generations before the Snake Sacrifice takes place (above, p. 51).

Chs. 33-35. Kadrū's second son, Vāsuki, King of the Snakes, responds to his mother's curse differently: he decides to do something about it. He calls a council of Snakes (much like the council of devils in *Paradise Lost*), who suggest ten methods for disrupting Janamejaya's sacrifice, each more whimsical and wicked than the one before. Vāsuki rejects them all. Finally, his brother Elāpatra reveals an escape clause in the curse: Brahmā approved the curse, he says, but declared that someday it would be cancelled by a man named Āstīka, born to a brahmin named Jaratkāru who marries a woman bearing the same name. Hearing this, Vāsuki sets out to fulfill these conditions, so that the Snakes can be saved.

Having helped to churn the ocean, Vāsuki approaches Brahmā and asks a boon. Here too the order of events is confusing: which came first, the churning, or the curse? Van Buitenen reads, "Not too long a time had passed since all the Gods and Asuras churned Varuṇa's ocean" (96), implying (logically) that Brahmā already owed Vāsuki a boon. Dutt and Ganguli, however, report that the churning came *after* Elāpatra's speech:

> Not long after this [Elāpatra's speech], the Devas and the Asuras churned the abode of Varuna (Ocean). (Dutt, 64)

That, of course, makes no sense chronologically, because (as in the case of Śeṣa) that would put the churning of the ocean both before and after Kadrū's curse. Confusing? Yes, and the same story is told again only a few chapters later, by Jaratkāru to her son Āstīka, and in that telling it is clear even in van Buitenen's translation that her curse does indeed come both before and after the churning.

> "The God Grandfather of the worlds himself heard her curse and consented to it, saying, 'So shall it be.'

> Vāsuki, however, on hearing Grandfather's word, sought refuge with the Gods, my son, when the Elixir was churned from the ocean.
> And the celestials, once they had gained their desire and obtained the incomparable Elixir, gave my brother the place of honor and went to the Grandfather.
> All the Gods sought to appease him together with Vāsuki, 'Let that curse pass by King Vāsuki!'" (115)

Come to think of it, Garuḍa was also born both before and after the churning. And if the chronology were not already confused enough, Brahmā's reply to Vāsuki throws it even further out of joint:

> "I myself, O Immortals, was the one who inspired the speech that the Snake Elāpatra at the time recounted to him.
> Let the King of the Snakes carry out those words for which the time now has come. The evil Snakes are doomed to die, the law-abiding ones are not.
> The brahmin Jaratkāru has been born and is devoting himself to awesome austerities. When the time comes, Vāsuki must give him his sister Jaratkāru." (96)

How could Jaratkāru already be born? He is Āstīka's father, only one generation removed from the Snake Sacrifice itself, which takes place long after the Bhārata war, not in "the Eon of the Gods," right after the churning of the ocean. Clearly the poets have completely abandoned chronology—if they were ever following it. We are caught in what Hiltebeitel calls the poem's many "narrative experiments with time." (38)

Chs. 36-46. Now at last the Bard has returned to the story of Jaratkāru. We heard a short version of that story thirty pages ago, back in chapter thirteen, after which Śaunaka asked for the full version. Now, after twenty-three chapters of more or less necessary background, we are finally back. This time the story is told at great length—but no sooner does it begin than it is put off again for five more chapters—for first we must hear (at last) the story of how Janamejaya's father was killed by Takṣaka. This is the story Utanka mentioned to Janamejaya back in chapter three, some fifty pages ago. At the end of that chapter Janamejaya turned to his councilors and asked them for the story. We will return to that scene, but not until the story is told yet again, in chapter forty-five. The architectonics of the *Āstīka* story are not only complex, they are greatly distended. It is difficult to see the structure of a story that is interrupted for thirty or fifty pages at a time.

Taking stock again. As we move toward the climax of *Āstīka*, which will be the Snake Sacrifice itself, there are a number of plot lines in motion. The Bard is answering two related questions: (1) Why did Janamejaya hold his Snake Sacrifice, and (2) Why did Āstīka interrupt it? Each answer involves a set of immediate causes and a set of ultimate causes. Up to this point the Bard has been dwelling on the ultimate causes, the mythical ones, which involve the churning of the ocean: (1) the Snake Sacrifice was ordered by Kadrū, as part of her curse on her Snake children, and (2) Āstīka's intervention was ordered by Brahmā, as a boon to Vāsuki for helping to churn the ocean.

Now we are coming to the more immediate causes, the historical ones. (1) Janamejaya ordered the sacrifice because his father Parikṣit was killed by Takṣaka, as the result of a rash curse by a brahmin; and (2) Āstīka was born to stop the sacrifice, because (a) his father conceived him to save his brahmin ancestors, and (b) his mother bore him to save her brother Vāsuki and the other Snakes. All these stories are being woven together and gradually drawn into a single stream.

Western readers might ask, are these stories subplots of each other, as we expect from multiple plots in works like *The Odyssey* or *King Lear*? Are they variations on a theme, illuminating each other in some way? Or are their apparent variety and randomness somehow the point?

Also, what is the relation of the "historical" stories to the mythical ones, like the churning of the ocean and Garuḍa's quest? We are familiar with this sort of double causality in the *Iliad*, where human actions are ultimately caused by the gods, whether or not the human actors realize it. Hector's fate has to do with Paris, Achilles and Patroclus, but also, at the same time but on a different level, with Zeus, Hera and Thetis. The same "double agency" is found in many biblical stories—do Joseph's brothers sell him into slavery because they hate him, or is it God's providential plan to save the family? One difference between the *Iliad* and the Bible on the one hand, and the *Mahābhārata* on the other, however, is that the latter's mythical stories seem to belong to a primordial past, "long ago, in the Eon of the Gods." The curses, vows and predictions made then, which must by their nature come true, lead eventually to the sort of narrative paradoxes we find in modern time-travel literature.

Or so it seems; in the end, we may just have to rethink the nature of time and causality in the poem. Our concern for linear chronology may simply be inappropriate. As we have seen, events in mythical time cannot be ordered chronologically, or integrated neatly into the sequence of historical events. In any case, we should not assume that our poets think loosely or make mistakes on the subject of Time. Time, after all, is their theme.

Now, back to the narrative. Brahmā has just announced, much to our surprise, that Jaratkāru has already been born.

Ch. 36 begins with an odd moment in the outer frame: Śaunaka interrupts to ask for the etymology of the name Jaratkāru, and when the Bard provides one,

> Upon hearing this, the law-abiding Śaunaka started to laugh, and he complimented Ugraśravas, saying "that fits!" (97)

Van Buitenen writes in a note, "I do not see how this etymology can inspire merriment." (444) Hiltebeitel, however, dwells on the episode for three pages (174-76). The etymology that the Bard provides is obscure, and Hiltebeitel concludes (with an exclamation point) that he "has made it up for the occasion!" (175) And why is Śaunaka so delighted with it? Because, according to Hiltebeitel, Śaunaka is not just an interlocutor, but a true collaborator in the telling of the story—for Śaunaka, as we will learn hundreds of pages later, is, like Vyāsa, a character in the main narrative of the *Mahābhārata*. He appears three times in Book Three as an advisor to Yudiṣṭhira. So he too is a long-lived seer and a witness to the events. As Vyāsa links the main narrative to the inner frame, Śaunaka links it to the outer frame. That is why his hermitage is an appropriate setting for a retelling of the story, and that is why he already knows the story that the Bard tells. Here we see Śaunaka good-humoredly testing the Bard's ability to make the parts of the great story "fit." It is not such an easy job, as I myself have been discovering in trying just to summarize the poem.

The Story of Parikṣit—at Last. That moment of etymological merriment occupies only a few *śloka*s, and then with a sudden transition—"Then, upon another time, there was a

King Parikṣit" (97)—we are plunged into the story of Parikṣit's death. We were actually expecting the story of Jaratkāru, but the Bard will deliver both of these long-delayed stories simultaneously, as it were. The next ten chapters are extremely confusing in form, if not in content, as we shift back and forth between the two stories. To summarize it ahead of time:

> **Chs. 36-40.** The Bard tells Śaunaka (at last) the story of how Takṣaka killed Parikṣit.
> **Chs. 41-44.** Then he tells (again) the story of how Jaratkāru saved his ancestors by marrying Jaratkāru, this time adding how he later left her, and why their son was named Āstīka.
> **Chs. 45-46.** Then Śaunaka asks to hear the Parikṣit story *again*, this time just as Janamejaya heard it from his councilors; so the Bard tells it again, this time not in his own voice, but as the councilors told it.

Why is the Parikṣit story repeated after only a few chapters? We would like to believe that such repetition is purposeful and meaningful, but this repetition is not as easy to understand as others we have seen in the poem—for example the Jaratkāru story, which was first told in summary and then at greater and greater length. We have become accustomed to repetitions of that sort; but in this case the same story is being told differently by different narrators, or at least in different voices by the same narrator, as if to different audiences. It is the sort of repetition we are familiar with in Western works like the Bible, *Beowulf* or *The Sound and the Fury*. To a Western critic, then, it seems natural to compare the two versions of the Parikṣit story, before considering the Jaratkāru story that is sandwiched between them.

We have been waiting to hear the story of Parikṣit since the end of *Pauṣya*, thirty-three chapters ago. There Utanka, in order to prompt Janamejaya to perform the Snake Sacrifice, told him that his father had been killed by the Snake Takṣaka. Now, thirty-three chapters later, the Bard finally tells Śaunaka that story, before he returns to that point in his narrative where Janamejaya asked to hear it from his councilors in order to decide whether to perform the sacrifice.

Reader be warned. The twice-told story of Parikṣit's death strongly foreshadows the climax of *Āstīka* at the Snake Sacrifice. Both narratives end in last-second cliffhanger contests between Takṣaka and first Parikṣit, then his son Janamejaya, each of whom has isolated himself in a ritual space. There is a very loud echo effect at the end of *Āstīka*, and it is easy to confuse the details of the two stories—the death of Parikṣit, and the interruption of Janamejaya's Snake Sacrifice—in our memory. But before we encounter that confusion, let us confront another one, comparing the two versions of the Parikṣit story.

The first version (chs. 36-40). As the Bard tells the story the first time, King Parikṣit pursues a deer into a forest, and comes upon a brahmin. He asks him if he has seen the deer, but the brahmin says nothing. The king does not realize that the brahmin has taken a vow of silence. Angry, the king hangs a dead snake around the brahmin's shoulders and departs. This is clearly a dreadful breach of ritual purity, but the brahmin remains at perfect peace. His irascible son, however, when he learns from a friend how the king has treated his father, declares, "Beware the power of my austerities!" (98). He pronounces a terrible curse upon the king, whom he calls a "despiser of the brahmins": the king, he proclaims, shall be killed by the Snake Takṣaka in just seven days.

The ethical point of the story then follows, and it comes as a bit of a surprise:

> Thereupon the father said to his furious son,
> "You have done me no kindness, son. This is not the Law of ascetics. We are living in the realm of this mighty king
> and we are protected by him in accordance with the Laws. I do not approve of his crime, yet our like must always and in every way condone the ruling king, son.
> The Law that is hurt, hurts back. Were the king not to protect us, we should be severely oppressed;
> we should not be able to live the Law as we desire... Give up your anger, or give up the Law.
> For the anger of ascetics kills the merit they have painfully gathered, and deprived of the merits of Law, their course becomes evil." (99)

"Give up your anger, or give up the Law." That is, brahmins must never give in to anger, which is a kṣatriyan weakness. Rash curses spoken in anger have been the most persistent motif in all these stories. Once uttered, they cannot be retracted, and they also cannot fail to come true. It is not too surprising, then, when the son responds,

> "If I have acted rashly, father, or if I have done a wrong, or whether it pleases or displeases you, the word I have spoken will not be belied!
> It shall never be altered, here I stand and tell you, father. I do not speak idly even when joking, let alone when cursing!" (99)

The father sends word to the king, warning him of his son's curse. Parikṣit, terrified, has his palace built on a pillar to protect himself from Snakes.

There follows one of the most perplexing episodes in the whole of *Āstīka*; for who arrives on the seventh day to save Parikṣit from Takṣaka, but Kaśyapa!

> "When the King of the Snakes has bitten him, I shall cure him of his fever," so he reflected, "and I will earn wealth and merit." (101)

Remember, Kaśyapa is a long-lived brahmin seer like Vyāsa and Śaunaka. We noted earlier that he is also a demiurge, like Bhṛgu; and we learned, way back in chapter thirteen, that when Brahmā approved Kadrū's curse on the Snakes, Kaśyapa was given the secret of healing their poison. That would seem to be the point of his appearing now. Oddly, however, there is no mention here of his being Takṣaka's father. Van Buitenen notes that his name is spelled slightly differently in this episode (Kāśyapa, not Kaśyapa), so perhaps this is a different Kaśyapa, perhaps a descendent, a member of the clan, since the new spelling is a patronymic, meaning "son or descendant of Kaśyapa." In any case, as he heads for Hāstinapura to save Parikṣit, he is stopped by Takṣaka, who challenges him. The brahmin replies by promptly demonstrating that he can save *anything* from snakebite, even a tree!—and so, Takṣaka simply agrees to pay him off.

> Kāśyapa said:
> "I am going there for riches. You give them to me, Snake, and then I shall return home, most eminent Serpent."
> Takṣaka said:

"Whatever riches you seek from that king, I shall give you more today. Turn back, great brahmin!"

The Bard said:

The good brahmin Kāśyapa heard Takṣaka's word, and being wise as well as puissant, reflected upon the king. Since the powerful Kāśyapa was gifted with second sight,

he knew that the life of this king of the Pāṇḍava's line had to come to an end. Thus the great hermit took from Takṣaka all the wealth he wanted and turned back. (102)

Our first impression is that Kāśyapa has betrayed the king, but first impressions can be misleading. It may be that being prescient, he knows how the story will end, and, realizing that he cannot change the ending, takes his leave, tricking Takṣaka into giving him what looks like a bribe. Is Kāśyapa to be blamed for this? It seems not.

Takṣaka then proceeds to the city disguised as a brahmin, and sends some fruit to the king.

As the king was about to eat the fruit with his ministers, O Śaunaka, there appeared a small worm in the fruit he had taken,

quite tiny with black eyes, and the color of copper. Picking it up, the grand king said to his ministers,

"The sun is setting, and I have no more danger to fear from poison. Now let the hermit's word come true—this worm may bite me!

It shall be Takṣaka himself, so that a lie be averted." The councilors, prompted by Time, applauded him.

> And having spoken, the king placed the little worm on his throat and, doomed to die and robbed of his senses, gave a quick laugh.
>
> He was still laughing when Takṣaka coiled around him—he had come out of the fruit that the king had been given. (103)

Why on earth does the king hold the worm to his throat? Because if he names the worm Takṣaka, the brahmin's curse can be fulfilled in some technical way, even as it is being obviated, "so that a lie be averted." The brahmin's curse, remember, cannot *not* be fulfilled. The only question is whether the king is clever enough to perform such a substitution himself; and the answer is, obviously not.

The second version (chs. 45-46). The second version of this story, told only five chapters later, differs from the first in several respects. Here the Bard adapts the story to the way Janamejaya would have heard it from his councilors. In this version, the councilors place more blame on Parikṣit: the dispute between the father and son hermits is absent, including the speech praising tolerance of kings. Kāśyapa's secret motives for accepting the "bribe" are also absent, making it look as if the brahmin did indeed simply betray the king.

Is the story being "brahminized" by the brahmins telling it? If so, then it is partly at the expense of the brahmins in it. On closer inspection, it looks as if the councilors are subtly trying to dissuade Janamejaya from taking revenge against Takṣaka, even as they appear to urge him on. If that is the case, their ploy seems to work, because after finally hearing this story, Janamemaya still cannot bring himself to proclaim the Snake Sacrifice. He demands more details. The councilors say,

"This is the gruesome history that we now have told you entire and complete, as it was seen and heard, good king.

Now that you have heard, herdsman of men, how the king was vanquished and the seer Utanka insulted, you must dispose of the immediate future."

Janamejaya said:

"I first wish to hear what was said between the King of the Snakes and Kāśyapa in that forest, which must have been empty of people.

By whom was it witnessed and who heard what came to your ears? When I have heard that, I shall set my mind on the destruction of the Snakes."

The Councilors said:

"Sire, listen to the tale that someone has told us about the encounter on the road between this prince among brahmins and this Prince of the Snakes.

A certain man had been looking for dead branches to use as kindling wood for a sacrifice and had climbed up that tall tree.

The Snake and brahmin were unaware of him sitting in the tree, and he was burned to ashes along with the tree itself:

the power of the brahmin brought both him and the tree back to life, good king. Afterward he came here and told his story in the city.

What we told you about the encounter of Takṣaka and the brahmin was precisely as it happened and was witnessed." (112)

How clever of Janamejaya to notice that part of the story he had been told had no witness, and thus no obvious authority. Once that is cleared up, however, it is now obvious that

Kāśyapa could indeed have cured Parikṣit's snakebite—which makes Takṣaka's bribe seem even more invidious. Having squeezed this extra bit of information out of his (reluctant?) councilors, Janamejaya finally makes up his mind to go ahead with the sacrifice. He offers three reasons for doing so: (1) his father was killed by Takṣaka; (2) Utanka was insulted by Takṣaka; and especially, (3) Kāśyapa was bribed by Takṣaka.

> "It was the Snake's blindness that made him stop that good brahmin Kāśyapa, who had come to return his life to the unvanquished king.
> This is the great transgression of the evil Takṣaka: that he gave riches to the brahmin lest he gave life back to the king!
> To please Utanka, and to please greatly myself and all of you, I shall go and avenge my father!" (112)

But what kind of reasoning is this? Is it wicked to *offer* a bribe, but good to *accept* one? Is it possible that Janamejaya is making a mistake here? Yes—for in the end the whole Snake Sacrifice will be revealed to be a mistake. Janamejaya's reasons for holding it appear to be almost willful misinterpretations of the stories he has been told.

Before we proceed to the story of Jaratkāru, there is an important note to add about Parikṣit. We have now heard about his death in some detail, twice; but we have heard nothing about his birth. That is surprising, because although we may have no reason to suspect it at this point, we will eventually learn that he is by no means a minor character in the epic. His birth, in fact, is a key event in the epic as a whole. When the great battle is finally over, and an ultimate weapon is loosed upon the Pāṇḍavas, killing all their progeny and ending their line, Kṛṣṇa reveals a prophecy:

> "'When the Kuru lineage fails, a son shall be born to you, and he shall be Parikṣit even while still in the womb.'
> 'The words of that virtuous man will indeed come true, and Parikṣit will be the son who re-establishes the Pāṇḍava line." (X.16, Smith 578-79)

Six chapters of Book XIV (64-69) will be given over to the account of Parikṣit's miraculous birth—but at this point in the frame story there is no reference to his role in the *Mahābhārata*.

We have a right to be pleasantly surprised that the poet or narrator—ostensibly Vyāsa or Vaiśaṃpāyana—really does allow the narrative to unfold consecutively, notwithstanding the many summaries embedded in the poem, and despite the aphorism that no one ever reads it for the first time. Even though the audience always already knows the whole story, the narrator seldom spoils our suspense by looking ahead more than a few chapters. The only early hints of Parikṣit's role in the main narrative that I can find, and they are very slight, are a single *śloka* in one of the opening summaries (42) and another in a genealogy later in Book I (214).

The Story of Jaratkāru—at Last. "In the meantime, Jaratkāru the ascetic traversed the entire earth" (103). Sandwiched between the two versions of the Parikṣit story we find (at long last) the story of the two Jaratkārus and the birth of Āstīka, this time told full length, richly textured with all the usual puzzles and paradoxes.

After Jaratkāru's encounter with his ancestors in the cave (now fully allegorized as Time), and his marriage to Vāsuki's sister, the story continues with a subtle dispute between the brahmin husband and his new Snake wife (involving yet another rash vow), which explains the origin and meaning of the name Āstīka. Jaratkāru makes a terrible vow to his new wife Jaratkāru:

> "Never do or say aught that displeases me. I shall abandon thee and my lodgings in thy house if thou ever causest me displeasure. Mark this word that I have spoken!" (106)

Common sense tells us that this demand is impossible. And indeed, on one occasion when she wakes him in time to worship the setting sun, he is displeased, claiming,

> "I know in my heart, woman with the shapely thighs, that the sun does not have the courage to set at its appointed time while I am asleep!" (107)

There is an example of brahmin ontological arrogance! Sobbing, she begs him to stay, because she needs to bear a child by him to save the Snakes. He, knowing she is pregnant even before she does, touches her belly and says, "There is" ("*Asti*"), as he walks out the door. Hiltebeitel thinks the moment metaphysical, echoing throughout the epic (162-3). Doniger says:

> "his name is an obvious contrast with the better-known designation, Nāstika, 'One who says it is not,' the usual Hindu word for a heretic. Astika's story is therefore the story of the affirmation of good religion (in which one does not sacrifice snakes)." (O'Flaherty 19)

We would like to think that the parallel stories of Parikṣit and Jaratkāru are related thematically—as, for example, Telemachus's voyage mirrors Odysseus's, or Gloucester's tragedy mirrors Lear's; but except for the fact that Āstīka, Takṣaka and Janamejaya will all come together at the sacrifice, their stories are remarkably independent, more like the random interweaving plots of *Don Quixote* or *War and Peace*.

12. The Sacrifice—At Last
(*Āstīka*, Chapters 47-53)

If the frame story of the Snake Sacrifice is a long preamble to the *Mahābhārata*, everything we have read so far has been a long preamble to the Snake Sacrifice. Now at last the sacrifice can begin. The narrative will now run smoothly and quickly to the end of *Āstīka*, but we have no right to expect simplicity. Kadrū's curse must be fulfilled, but Brahmā's boon must also be fulfilled. The human characters are caught in this contradiction; there are a number of surprises and great suspense as they play out their contradictory destinies.

Ch. 47. Janamejaya moves swiftly to arrange the sacrifice. His priests inform him,

> "Sire, there is a great Session that the Gods have devised for you. The Ancient Lore describes it with the name of the Session of the Snakes.
>
> No one but you, overlord of men, can be the officer of this Session, thus declare the masters of the Lore; and we possess this rite." (113)

They seem to know the story of the curse, then, but do they also know that the sacrifice will be interrupted? For some reason that knowledge belongs not to the priests, but to a bard named Lohitākṣa.

> Now earlier, when the Session of the Snakes was yet to begin, there appeared a great portent that predicted that the sacrifice would be disrupted.
>
> As the sacrificial terrain was being laid out, a master builder of much wisdom and well versed in the arts of build-

ing spoke up. This Holder of the Cord, who was a bard of the ancient Lore, said:

"Seeing the place and time that the measuring was carried out, I say the sacrifice will not be concluded, a brahmin being the cause."

Whereupon the king, before the time of his consecration, ordered the steward, "Let no one enter who is unknown to me!" (113)

Lohitākṣa has detected a fault in the ritual, something inauspicious having to do with the construction of the sacrificial site; but he seems not to know the story of Brahmā's boon to Vāsuki. We have seen enough curses, vows and predictions, however, to know that Lohitākṣa's prediction is likely to have a binding force of its own. It will be yet another "cause" for the climactic action. The king, of course, tries to prevent the prediction from coming true, just as his father tried to protect himself from Takṣaka by living on a pillar, but to no avail.

Now the sacrifice begins. Snakes pour into the sacrificial fire:

The snakes began to drop into the blazing flames, writhing and wretched and crying out to one another.

They darted and hissed and wildly coiled about with tails and heads as they fell into the radiant fires—

white, black, blue, old and young—screeching terrifying screams, they fell into the high blazing flames,

hundreds of thousands and millions and tens of millions of the Snakes ... fell into the fire, punished by their mother's curse. (113-14)

Chs. 48-50. After the chief priests are named, and the horror of the burning snakes is described further, the narrative turns to Takṣaka, who is the real target of the sacrifice. In the other world he seeks out Indra, who, with Brahmā's permission, offers him protection.

Takṣaka's brother Vāsuki, however, is not protected, and he falls into a fever from the heat of the sacrificial flames. Mythical space is just as peculiar as mythical time: no matter "where" Vāsuki is, he feels the heat of the sacrifice. It is finally time, he tells his sister Jaratkāru, to tell Āstīka why he was born.

So Jaratkāru gives her son a quick summary of the whole story of the churning of the ocean, the wager of the sisters, the curse, and Brahmā's boon; whereupon, Āstīka dutifully rushes off to stop the sacrifice—but is stopped by the keepers of the gate—for of course Janamejaya has been expecting just such an intrusion.

As the plot reaches its greatest intensity, van Buitenen suddenly switches from prose to verse. That is because certain passages in the *Mahābhārata* are not written in *śloka*s but in a more elevated meter, the *triṣṭubh*, which Van Buitenen translates in verse. The only other time he has done so up to this point is back in *Pauṣya*, when Utanka pursued Takṣaka into the underworld to retrieve his earrings. There Utanka tried to trick Takṣaka by singing an elegant hymn of praise to him. Āstīka now uses the same trick. Chapter fifty consists of his long, beautiful hymn to the Snake Sacrifice, praising Vyāsa, the priests, the flame and Janamejaya in turn. Van Buitenen's talents as a translator and poet are evident:

> Great-spirited Fire, the Many-Splendored,
> The Widely Radiant, the Golden-Spermed,
> All-Eating, South-Crested, whose Trail is Blackened,

Now longs for the offering, to eat it, the God. (117)

Ch. 51. The ruse works. We, of course, realize that all of Āstīka's praise is ironic, but the king, dazzled by his song, impulsively decides to grant him a boon. The priests and *sadasyas* object, however, because Takṣaka has not yet been burned. Lohitākṣa, "the great-spirited Bard well-versed in the Lore," explains that Takṣaka is being protected by Indra; so the king demands (with kṣatriyan arrogance) that the priests make Indra himself appear! And suddenly, "Indra himself thereupon appeared,"

In puissance great, on a chariot mounted,
While the praise of the Gods surrounded him,
And trailing a wake of mighty clouds
And crowds of aerial spirits and nymphs.

The Snake was tucked in the hem of his robe,
But he found no shelter and was greatly alarmed.
Quoth the king to his priests who knew the spells,
Waxing angry and set on Takṣaka's death:

Janamejaya said:
"Priests! If Takṣaka the Snake is in Indra's keeping, then hurl him into the fire with Indra himself!" (119)

Indra then drops Takṣaka, who falls from the sky toward the fire; but before he reaches it the priests announce, most surprisingly,

"Thy sacrifice, lord among kings, is working toward its proper end. Now thou mayest grant a boon to the worthy brahmin." (120)

What are they thinking? Are they being over-hasty, like the king? How could they not know what boon Āstīka will demand? Again, however, appearances can be deceiving; perhaps they know exactly what they are doing. In any case, Āstīka gets his boon—which is, of course, that the sacrifice be stopped—before Takṣaka burns. The king, immediately realizing his mistake, asks Āstīka to choose another boon, but

> thereupon the *sadasyas*, knowing their Veda, all said to the king: "The brahmin must have his boon." (120)

What an interesting and puzzling development! Only moments ago these same *sadasyas* objected to the idea of the king granting Āstīka a boon, because Takṣaka had not yet been burned. They knew Āstīka would interrupt the sacrifice. Moments later, however, with Takṣaka still not burned, and Āstīka having confirmed their suspicion, suddenly they insist on granting the boon. The king's haste was obviously an error, but their sudden reversal seems calculated. Still, if this is the outcome they wanted all along, why did they object in the first place?

Brahmins are caught in an awkward position, having to obey the king and advise him at the same time. This episode illustrates the complexity inherent in the formula we emphasized early on:

> Vyāsa's "Vedic" instruction of Janamejaya on his proper action in the world, and the brahman community's monitoring of that instruction represented the ancient Indian complementarity between *brahman* and *kṣatra*—transcendent wisdom and governmental power. (Fitzgerald, 169)

The poets have kept the tension high, the motives obscure, and the action fast-paced and confused; but in the end, of course, the outcome is inevitable: the sacrifice must be stopped. That was declared by the gods, eons ago.

Chs. 52-53. Just at this point, as Takṣaka hangs above the fire, Śaunaka, way out in the outer frame, interrupts the Bard again, asking him to recite the names of all the Snakes who were killed in the sacrifice.

Here we have a fine literary joke at the very climax of the story. We want to know, will the king grant Āstīka's boon? Will Takṣaka be saved at the last moment? But we must wait to find out, while the Bard patiently complies with Śaunaka's request by naming eighty-eight of the millions of Snakes incinerated, the most famous of those who died, all carefully organized genealogically. More than thirty *śloka*s will go by before we return to the action, at which point the narrative will pick up right where it left off. Before the action resumes, however, the Bard goes on to explain how it is that Takṣaka could remain hanging in the air above the fire for so long. Here is another of the poem's "narrative experiments with time." We are told that Takṣaka could only remain suspended over the fire during the long catalogue of names because Āstīka shouted "Stay! Stay!" three times,

> And the Snake stood still in the air with fluttering heart, as
> a body would stand still in a circle of bulls. (122)

That is, Āstīka, who is a character in the story, seems to realize that the sacrifice must be interrupted for a few minutes while the Bard who is telling the story, long afterward in the Naimiṣa Forest, takes time for a digression. It is as if, when we pause a film, the characters in it shout to each other to hold their positions—in mid-air—until the projector is turned back on. It is a joke worthy of Cervantes: Quixote knows he is a character in a book, and sometimes attributes the surprising events in his life to "the wise man whose task it will be to write the history of my deeds" (139). We are also familiar with the idea in modern works like Pirandello's *Six Characters in Search of an Author*, or Woody Allen's *Purple Rose of Cairo*.

Is it too much to believe that the epic poets of ancient India could create a character who realizes he is actually in a story being told aloud by someone else? We have only to remember how the author Vyāsa intervenes in the epic's action "like a film director stepping onto the set," as we noted earlier. *The Rāmāyaṇa* has a similar twist: as Quixote reads the very book he is in, so Rāma has the *Rāmāyaṇa* read to him, its hero, within the *Rāmāyaṇa* itself. The Indian epics overbrim with such "modern" or postmodern narrative effects.

Now, back to the action. Once it resumes, Janamejaya says,

> "Let his wish be done, even as Āstīka has demanded.
> This sacrifice must be brought to an end, and the Snakes shall be safe. Let Āstīka be pleased, and let also the Bard's prediction come true!"
> There was a joyous tumult of cheers when Āstīka was granted his boon, and the sacrifice of King Pāṇḍaveya, son of Parikṣit, was ended.
> King Janamejaya Bhārata was greatly pleased and gave to the priests and *sadasyas* who had gathered there fees of riches by the hundred and thousands.
> Also, he gave much wealth to the Bard Lohitākṣa, the builder who had predicted that a brahmin would become the cause that the sacrifice was stopped. (122)

Everyone, including Janamejaya, is delighted that the sacrifice has been interrupted. But why? Understanding this sudden reversal may be the greatest of all our interpretive challenges in the frame narrative. Is it not as if Priam were delighted by Troy's defeat, and handed out lavish rewards to all those who had predicted it?

Oddly, we are never told what happens to Takṣaka. He has been rescued in the nick of time, but it is as if he hangs suspended over the fire even today. Perhaps it is not important what happens to him; perhaps stopping the sacrifice is the important thing. However, Minkowski and others have seen in his rescue an important parallel with the main story of the *Mahābhārata*, which may reveal the ultimate relevance of the frame story.

> Embedding the epic in an apocalyptic rite that only some survive prefigures the theme of the epic as a whole: the passing of an age, the eradication of a race, the survival of a few. Parikṣit is the sole survivor of the bygone era in the following age. He was saved by the intervention of Krishna. That he should be killed by Takṣaka, who is then saved from another holocaust by another intervention, this time by Āstīka, makes the two stories interlock. (397)

Jatavallabhula too, in her treatment of the war as a sacrifice, a *raṇa-sattra*, sees connections between the Bhṛgu myth of Rāma's near-eradication of the kṣatriya class, the great Bhārata war which accomplishes the same thing, and the Snake Sacrifice:

> We might see a brahmanical construct in the stories pertaining to the destruction of the *kṣatriyas*... In this connection, we might draw a parallel with the snake sacrifice

> (*sarpa-sattra*) performed by Janamejaya... Thus ultimately the nearly total destruction of the kṣatriyas, just like that of the snakes, is viewed as a means of restoring *dharma*. (95-96)

The connection is right, but her conclusion is only half-right; for if destroying the Snakes is a means of restoring *dharma*, then so is saving a remnant at the last minute. In the end we must try to understand how Āstīka's rescue of the Snakes, including Takṣaka, serves *dharma*.

The sacrifice over, Āstīka returns to the world of the Snakes, who are so relieved to have been saved from destruction that they offer him a boon. And what is his wish? That anyone who recounts the story we have just heard should be safe from Snakes! The Bard concludes,

> "Thus I have recited to you truthfully the Epic of Āstīka.
> And when one has recited, or one has listened to this
> Epic of Āstīka, which is most conducive to the Law
> and increasing merit, O brahmin, these illustrious exploits
> of the sage Āstīka from their very beginning, he shall
> nowhere encounter any danger from the Snakes." (123)

13. Rereading

Having read the frame stories as closely as we have, now we can read them again with greater comprehension and pleasure. They were told, remember, to an audience that already knew them. It was of *The Epic of Āstīka* that Śaunaka said to the Bard, "Tell this tale as your father used to tell it!" (71) Now we too already know the story.

Looking back over these fifty-three chapters, three plot elements leap out as especially puzzling. (1) How could this entire vast and intricate plot turn on something as trivial as a wager over the color of a horse's tail? (2) Why the obsession with Snakes? And (3) how are we to understand Janamejaya's sudden reversal in the end?

The first question has no very conspicuous answer. Gambling is a common metaphor for fate, but Uccaiḥśravas is not presented as having a powerful mythical role, as Garuḍa is, for example. He is the king of horses, and the horse of Indra; but if he symbolizes some natural or supernatural force in this story, like the horse that Utanka blows into, we are not told what it is. The object of the sisters' wager seems a bit arbitrary, then, like the earrings Utanka has to fetch.

What is at stake in the case of the horse Uccaiḥśravas? He disappears from the narrative as soon as the wager is made. He is legendarily white, so obviously Vinatā should have won the bet. The mother of Snakes is clearly a deceiver—and yet the Snakes themselves pay a bigger price for her deceit than her victim Vinatā does. Are Snakes evil, then? According to the gods, yes and no. In the world of myth nothing is ever just black or white—perhaps that itself is the meaning of the episode. If we are disappointed at not having a more rational explanation of Uccaiḥśravas's role in *Āstīka*, perhaps we are not yet willing to accept the full irrationality of myth.

As for the obsession with Snakes, a quick proof of how much we have learned to this point will be to read, now at last, the two and a half pages that van Buitenen devoted to these chapters in his Introduction (2-4). His highly compressed argument, which we should now be able to find comprehensible, turns out to be such a "strong" reading of the story that we may feel quite free to disagree with it. Van Buitenen is one of those scholars concerned with the question, Is there any history in these stories? He says, "I consider it likely that in this initial setting of a twelve-year session the memory of such a grandiose, though abortive, enterprise survives" (2-3); also, "The entire long *Book of Āstīka* serves to establish that a Snake Sacrifice was in fact held by King Janamejaya, a descendant of the Pāṇḍava heroes"(3). These are the assertions of a historian, not a literary critic, and they lead to a highly dubious literary conclusion:

> The *Book of Āstīka* not only authenticates Janamejaya's sacrifice as the setting of Vaiśaṃpāyana's recitation of the epic: it also reconfirms the evil of the snakes. This pouring on of hatred for the snakes through *Pauṣya, Puloman*, and *Āstīka* is extremely effective in helping us to accept the historical reality of Janamejaya's Snake Sacrifice: and effective it had to be made, for to the ancient Indians, among whom the non-Aryans must be counted, such a sacrifice must have been an abomination. (4)

This conclusion is as lopsided as Jatavallabhula's. Nothing in the poem is so black and white. Janamejaya is by no means the object of undiluted praise, nor are the Snakes the object of undiluted hatred. The Snakes do not deserve their mother's curse, as both Indra and Brahmā agree. There are good and bad Snakes. The Snakes helped the gods churn the ocean, after all. Would the Snake Sacrifice, if it had been completed, have ended with the death of Ananta too, on whom the whole world rests? Āstīka too, remember, is a Snake; and if Doniger is right, his name implies "the affirmation of good religion."

By the end of chapter forty-six Janamejaya has convinced himself that all Snakes are evil and must be killed; but the epic has painstakingly displayed every accident, irony, misunderstanding and error in his thinking, every weakness in his kṣatriyan motives, and has offered a superior brahmin ethic of *ahiṃsā* to trump his anger and violence.

With this superior brahmin ethic of *ahiṃsā* in mind, perhaps we can now understand Janamejaya's reversal. The universal applause that greets the failure of the sacrifice tells us that Janamejaya has finally accepted this brahmin wisdom, even if he had to be tricked into it. He now knows as well as the rest of ancient India does, that such a sacrifice "must have been an abomination"—not because the Snakes are evil, as van Buitenen suggests, but because the violence of the sacrifice itself is evil.

Understanding the rescue of the Snakes as a victory for *ahiṃsā*, involves us in another scholarly controversy, for it is not clear why or when non-violence might have emerged as an ethic for brahmins, much less for the other classes. Schmidt begins an article on "The Origin of *Ahiṃsā*" by quoting this deceptively clear testimony:

> According to Manu *ahiṃsā* is the duty of all the four classes (*varṇa*): "Non-injury, truth, non-stealing, purity, control of the senses—this Manu has declared to be the comprehensive law for the four classes." (628, citing Manu 10.63)

But how did this come to be? And what relation does this clear doctrine have to the confusing situation we see in the *Mahābhārata*? We have had occasion earlier to quote Hiltebeitel's pregnant conclusion on this issue: "The epic resists the universalization of ahiṃsā" (207); and we have only to think of Kṛṣṇa's advice to Arjuna in the *Bhagavad-Gītā*, that he must fight, to realize that the epic's attitude toward *ahiṃsā* is complex. So complex, in fact, that those who study the problem of the origin of *ahiṃsā* tend to avoid the evidence of the *Mahābhārata*, even though the frame story of the Snake Sacrifice seems to address it quite directly.

The most popular theory of the origin of *ahiṃsā* is summarized by Bodewitz:

> The heretic religions of Buddhism and Jainism which reacted against Vedism, had a rather strict application of the *ahiṃsā* rule, especially for the monks. Since Vedism is dominated by the ritual and in several sacrifices animals are killed as victims, one might suppose that the *ahiṃsā* doctrine had its roots in the rejection of the bloody sacrifices of Vedism. (20)

Although Bodewitz himself demurs on this last point, the theory he refers to seems to offer something like a master key to the story of Āstīka. In the world of the *Mahābhārata* there is a lively dispute between Vedic ritualists and ascetic anti-ritualists. Remember how Jaratkāru's ancestors demanded he give up his austerities and have a child; the Bard praised him for returning to Vedic practice:

> The Gods he satisfied with sacrifices of various stipends,
> the seers with his scholarship, and his ancestors with progeny. (71)

And yet his wife Jaratkāru has a son precisely for the purpose of stopping an animal sacrifice. Remember too how back in *Puloman* the Snake taught Ruru that *ahiṃsā* is a higher Law than Vedism:

> Not to inflict hurt, to speak the truth, and to be forgiving is assuredly for the brahmin a Law even higher than preserving the Veda." (63)

If it is true that *ahiṃsā* as an ethical law was born from the rejection of animal sacrifices, then it is no accident that the Snake Sacrifice of our frame story ends with the triumph of *ahiṃsā*. If the frame narrative is "about" anything, it is about stopping a Vedic animal sacrifice on the grounds that it is violent. How could it not be *hiṃsā*? Biardeau says that violence "cannot be called *hiṃsā* if [it] is not for the sake of killing but intended as sacrifice." (93) The Snake Sacrifice may be a sacrifice in one sense, in the older, Vedic ritual sense, but it is obvious that it is performed solely for the sake of killing Snakes; it has nothing to do with the later understanding of sacrifice as renunciation, or of war as a sacrifice. Arjuna's detachment in war qualifies his fighting as a sacrifice in the newer sense, and therefore as a form of *ahiṃsā*. Janamejaya's Snake Sacrifice, on the other hand, is not detached; it is merely *hiṃsā*, which is why it must be stopped.

Mikolajewska makes much the same point in "Good Violence Versus Bad: a Girardian Analysis of King Janamejaya's Snake Sacrifice," using the terminology of Rene Girard's *Violence and the Sacred* rather than the doctrine of *ahiṃsā*. She ties together the stories of Bṛgu, Garuḍa and the Snake Sacrifice as an illustration of Girard's theory about

> the necessity to block the "bad" violence of uncontrolled reprisal... by means of the controlled "good" violence of appropriate sacred ritual—which, alas, despite religion's meticulous care to distinguish the good from the bad, can all too easily degenerate... into "bad" violence all over again. (9-10)

The Snake Sacrifice, she says, is "an extreme example of the consequences of such confusion between 'good' violence and 'bad,' for the Snake Sacrifice "is in reality the worst kind of 'bad' violence... cloaked in the apparent respectability of a sacred sacrificial ritual." (49-50)

Reich has another approach to the forces at work in the sacrifice. She agrees that "the sacrificer, Janamejaya, is moved by desire for revenge and power, not by otherworldly goals" (149); but she explains that the *sattra* has a typically "agonistic" structure, in which interruption of the sacrifice can be understood as part of the sacrifice itself. At issue in this case is not only the relation of brahmins to Snakes, but the role of violence in sacrifice. She concludes,

> If war and sacrifice are two sides of the same coin, how can sacrifice claim transcendental value? The anxious suspicion that sacrifice and, by extension, the Brahman socioreligious order, dharma, is faulty because it is unavoidably founded on violence permeates... the Mahabharata as a whole. Not only the fascination but also the depth, the true greatness of the Mahabharata, lies precisely in the fact that it does not offer a single answer to the problem. The very concept of sacrifice and the understanding of the nature of sacrificial violence keep shifting in it. (168)

However you look at it, the triumph of *ahiṃsā* in *Āstīka* is only partial, because the gods declared the sacrifice no less clearly than they declared its interruption. The drama assumes balanced forces. The same is true of the Bhārata war. If the kṣatriya class must be destroyed yet again to restore *dharma*, it must also be renewed by a remnant. Janamejaya himself is the remnant. In that, ironically, he and Takṣaka have something in common.

If this "balance of forces," as I have called it, seems simply a contradiction at the heart of the epic, so be it. Doniger's overview of the history of Hinduism describes the *Mahābhārata* as essentially contradictory.

> The tradition has regarded it as a conversation among people who know one another's views and argue with silent partners. It is a contested text, a brilliantly orchestrated hybrid narrative with no single party line on any subject... The contradictions at its heart are not the mistakes of a sloppy editor but enduring dilemmas that no author could ever have resolved. (264)

Smith agrees: "With its usual all-embracing inclusiveness the *Mahābhārata* incorporates the differing views without seeking to reconcile them." On the issue of animal sacrifice, he notes that in Books 12 and 14, the poem "with magnificent inconsistency argues passionately on both sides." At one point in that debate, however (14.3),

> the narrator Vaiśaṃpāyana breaks off from his story to caution the listening Janamejaya—whose snake sacrifice he is attending at the time—against the sacrifice of animals. It may be significant that in both Books 12 and 14, it

> is the opponents of slaughter who have the last word. (lxii-lxiii).

So at least Vaiśaṃpāyana's position is clear—which is as close as we can ever hope to get, perhaps, to an authorial statement.

14. Coda: (*Āstīka*, chapters 53-56; Book XV, chapter 43; Book XVIII, chapter 5)

Āstīka is the epic's fifth "minor book." The sixth, *The Descent of the First Generations*, begins in the middle of chapter fifty-three. There Śaunaka thanks the Bard for the story of the Snake Sacrifice, and requests that he now recount the *Mahābhārata*, which was told during its intervals. We should know by now not to hold our breath. Since *Āstīka* contains no mention at all of how Vyāsa's great epic was performed during the sacrifice, the Bard now starts all over, right from the beginning.

In chapter fifty-four he recounts Vyāsa's arrival at the *sarpa-sattra*, which parallels the Bard's arrival at Śaunaka's *sattra* back in chapters one and three. After ablutions and gifts, Janamejaya requests from Vyāsa the story of the *Mahābhārata*. Vyāsa then turns to his student Vaiśaṃpāyana and asks him to tell it. Vaiśaṃpāyana quickly summarizes the entire *Mahābhārata* in chapter fifty-five, and then in chapter fifty-six Janamejaya naturally asks for the full version. The epic is finally about to begin. Vaiśaṃpāyana replies,

> "Of Vyāsa the great seer, whose puissance is boundless and whose fame is spread in all three worlds, I shall proclaim the thought entire.
>
> The epic that was here related by Satyavatī's son of boundless heat has a hundred thousand couplets that bring bliss.
>
> A man who knows it and makes others listen to it, and also folk who listen to it, attain to the realm of Brahmā and become the equals of the Gods...
>
> Kṛṣṇa Dvaipāyana the sage rose daily for three years and created this marvelous story of *The Mahābhārata*.

> Bull among Bhāratas, whatever is here, on Law, on Profit, on Pleasure, and on Salvation, that is found elsewhere. But what is not here is nowhere else." (129-30)

That is the "perimeter" I chose at the beginning as the place to end this reader's guide. It will be nearly a hundred more pages before the main story really begins, but at least the frame stories have now been told. Any reader who has managed to navigate them to this point should be able confidently to launch his or her own boat onto the vast ocean of the *Mahābhārata*.

We have much to look forward to in the remaining ninety-seven percent of the poem, and having read even this far, much of it will seem strangely familiar. "The central structuring principle of the epic is a certain kind of repetition," Ramanujan says (421). The stories we have read, from the largest to the smallest, will continue echoing through hundreds, even thousands of pages. Ruru's wife Pramadvarā will come to mind when we read the story of Śakuntalā; the competition between Kadrū and Vinatā will come to mind when we read the competition between Gāndhārī and Kuntī; the hundred Kauravas will remind us of the hundred Snakes; the Snake Sacrifice itself will come to mind when the Kandava forest is burned at end of Book I, in another fruitless attempt to kill Takṣaka; in the twelfth book we will find a long debate on the role of violence in *sattras*—and so on, and so on. As we read, some story will always be coming to mind.

The closest Western analogue to such a "network of repetition" is the typology of the Bible. The similarity is a little deceptive, however, because India has its own vocabulary for the phenomenon. By "a certain kind of repetition," Ramanujan really means *karma*, rather than agency, human or divine, as Western characters typically experience it:

> Many characters undergo similar experiences... Thus the experiences are not bound to one character. It's as if action is released from character... It's as if there's a kind of autonomy of action. Once set into motion, the act chooses its personae, constitutes is agents. (437)

But we are getting ahead of ourselves. There are no necessary limits to the lines of thought we might still pursue, or the scholarship and criticism we might still read, to further enrich our reading and re-reading of these early chapters; but having reached our declared perimeter, we will stop here at the water's edge.

Closing the Frame. And yet, still, we are not quite done. Thousands of pages later, as the epic finally draws to a close, the outer and inner frames of Janamejaya's Snake Sacrifice and Śaunaka's Naimiṣa Forest *sattra* are reinvoked in some detail, and finally closed or not closed. For completeness, we should take note of these two passages.

Book XV, Ch. 43. Fifteen years after the great battle, Dhṛtarāṣṭra, Gāndhārī and Kuntī retire to the forest, and shortly thereafter the Pāṇḍavas visit them there. Vyāsa appears out of nowhere, and offers Dhṛtarāṣṭra a boon, which is to see once more all those who perished in the battle. Everyone rushes off to the Gānga, where the dead rise out of the water for an entire night, for a grand reunion with the living.

At this point in the story, Janamejaya interrupts to ask Vyāsa if he might see his father Parikṣit in the same way, and Vyāsa obliges. We can read the passage in Ganguli/Dutt, or in Smith. The text is the same, but Smith's translation is fresher:

> King Janamejaya, who was taking the final ritual bath to
> conclude his snake sacrifice, was filled with joy, and
> bathed his father as well as himself;

> then after bathing, the best heir of Bharata addresed Āstīka son of Jaratkāru, born in the line of the Yāyāvra Brahmins.
>
> "Āstīka, it seems to me that the sacrifice has produced marvels of many kinds, for now my father has appeared to me to destroy my grief."
>
> "Best heir of Kuru's line," answered Āstīka, "when a sacrifice is attended by that great ascetic Vyāsa, the ancient seer, the sacrificer conquers both heaven and earth.
>
> You have heard a wonderful narrative, heir of Pāṇḍu; you have reduced the snakes to ash; you have followed in your father's footsteps;
>
> through your truthfulness, O prince, I have even been able to save Takṣaka; you have honored all the seers, and seen your noble father's condition.
>
> By hearing this sin-destroying narrative you have gained immense merit, and by seeing that noble man you have untied the knots that oppressed your heart." (Smith, 749-50)

Āstīka describes the compromise resolution we witnessed back in Book I as a carefully balanced win-win.

Parikṣit's death was a climactic moment in Book I, but only in Book XIV is it finally made clear, in the story of his birth, how crucial he is to the plot of the epic. Janamejaya's vision of him here in Book XV is all the more poignant for that knowledge. Now, having untied the knots that oppressed his heart, he asks Vaiśaṃpāyana to finish the story.

Book XVIII, Ch. 5. In the final chapter of the Critical Edition, the voice of Ugraśravas (whom Smith calls "the Sūta," i.e., the Bard) re-emerges, bringing us back to the scene in the Naimiṣa Forest. For hundreds of pages we have been reading dialogue between Vaiśaṃpāyana and Janamejaya, but here at the end we are suddenly jolted back to the outer frame.

> [Vaiśaṃpāyana spoke:]
> I have now related in detail, radiant heir of Bharata, the tale of the Kauravas and Pāṇḍavas, entire and complete.
> The Sūta spoke:
> This was the tale that King Janamejaya heard that best of Brahmins tell in intervals during the sacrificial rite, and he was filled with the greatest wonder.
> Then the ritual priests completed that rite for him, and Āstīka rejoiced that he had saved the snakes from destruction in it.
> All the Brahmins were delighted with the fee-gifts given by the king; receiving honour from him they returned to their homes.
> As for King Janamejaya, after giving the priests leave to depart, he returned from Takṣaśilā to Hāstinapura, the City of the Elephant.
> I have now related the entire tale narrated by Vaiśaṃpāyana at Vyāsa's command during the king's snake sacrifice. (Smith, 789)

And that is it for the frame narratives. We have finally learned that the Snake Sacrifice took place in Takṣaśilā, but nothing more of Takṣaka's fate. The Critical Edition ends here, after just a few more verses. The Vulgate, however, goes on to add another chapter, once more in the voice of Vaiśaṃpāyana addressing Janamejaya—even though the sacrifice has ended and the king has returned to his capital. That is certainly odd. Is it narrated by Ugraśravas the Bard to the monks in the Naimiṣa Forest? That seems unlikely, since he was not present—and yet how could it not be? We are simply not told. How odd—how interesting—that our poets should have been so fastidious about closing the inner frame after all this time, like unfinished business, and yet—in the Vulgate at least—chose to leave the outer frame so conspicuously open. It would have taken so little to close it, simply by having Śaunaka say to Ugraśravas the Bard, on behalf of the whole audience, including us, "Thank you!"

Works Cited

The *Mahābhārata*

Brook, Peter, director, and Jean-Claude Carrière. *The Mahābhārata*, on 2 DVDs. Image Entertainment, 1989.

Buck, William, trans. *MahaBhārata*. NY: Meridian Books, 1987.

Chopra, B. R. and Ravi Chopra, producers and directors. *The Mahābhārata*, on 16 DVDs. B. R. TV, 1989.

Dutt, M. N. *A Prose English Translation of the Mahābhārata*, 7 vols. Delhi: Parimal Publications, 2003.

Ganguli, Kisari Mohan, trans. *The Mahābhārata*, 4 vols. New Delhi: Munsiram Manoharial, 2004.

Narasimhan, Chakravarthi V., trans. *The Mahābhārata*. NY: Columbia UP, 1988.

Smith, John D, trans. *The Mahābhārata*. NY: Penguin, 2009.

Sukthankar, V. S., et al, eds. *Mahābhārata: Critical Edition*, vol I. Poona: Bhandarkar Oriental Research Institute, 1933.

Van Buitenen, J. A. B, trans. *The Mahābhārata*, vol. 1. Chicago: U of Chicago P, 1973, vol. 3, 1978.

Secondary

Armstrong, Karen. *The Great Transformation: The Beginning of our Religious Traditions*. NY: Knopf, 2006.

Biardeau, Madeleine. "The Salvation of the King in the *Mahābhārata*." *Contributions to Indian Sociology, New Series* 15.1-2 (1981): 75-97.

Bodewitz, Henk W. "Hindu Ahiṃsā and its Roots." in *Violence Denied*. ed. J. Houben and K. Van Kooij. Leiden: J. J. Brill, 1999, pp. 17-44.

Bowles, Adam. *Dharma, Disorder and the Political in Ancient India: The Āpaddharmaparvan of the Mahābhārata*. Boston: Brill, 2007.

Cervantes, Miguel de. *Don Quixote*, trans. Edith Grossman. NY: Harper Collins, 2003.

Doniger, Wendy. *The Hindus: An Alternative History*. NY: Penguin, 2009.

Fitzgerald, James L. "The Great Epic of India as Religious Rhetoric: A Fresh Look at the '*Mahābhārata*.'" *Journal of the American Academy of Religion* 51 (1983): 611-30.

----------. "India's Fifth Veda: The *Mahābhārata*'s Presentation of Itself," in *Essays on the Mahābhārata*. ed. Arvind Sharma. Leiden: E. J. Brill, 1991, pp. 150-70.

----------. "The Many Voices of the *Mahābhārata*." *Journal of the American Oriental Society* 123.4 (2003): 803-18.

Goldman, Robert P. *Gods, Priests, and Warriors: The Bhṛgus of the Mahābhārata*. NY: Columbia UP, 1977.

Hiltebeitel, Alf. *Rethinking the Mahābhārata: A Reader's Guide to the Education of the Dharma King*. Chicago: U of Chicago P, 2001.

----------. "Not Without Subtales: Telling Laws and Truths in the Sanskrit Epics." *Journal of Indian Philosophy* 33 (2005): 455-511.

Jatavallabhula, Danielle Feller. "Raṇayajña: The *Mahābhārata* War as a Sacrifice." in *Violence Denied*. ed. J. Houben and K. Van Kooij. Leiden: J. J. Brill, 1999, pp. 69-103.

Mehta, Mahesh. "The Problem of the Double Introduction in the *Mahābhārata*." *Journal of the American Oriental Society* 93.4 (1973): 547-50.

Mikolajewska, B., with F.E.J. Linton. "'Good' Violence versus 'Bad': A Girardian Analysis of King Janamejaya's Snake Sacrifice and Allied Events." New Haven, CT: The Lintons' Video Press, 2004.

Minkowski, C. Z. "Janamejaya's *Sattra* And Ritual Structure." *Journal of the American Oriental Society* 109.3 (1989): 401-20.

----------. "Snakes, *Sattras*, and the *Mahābhārata*." in *Essays on the Mahābhārata*. ed. Arvind Sharma. Leiden: E. J. Brill, 1991, pp. 384-400.

----------. "The Interrupted Sacrifice and the Sanskrit Epics." *Journal of Indian Philosophy* 29 (2001): 169-86.

O'Flaherty, Wendy Doniger, "Horses and Snakes in the Ādi Parvan of the *Mahābhārata*." in *Aspects of India: Essays in Honor of Edward Cameron Dimock*. eds. Margaret Case and N. Gerald Barrier. New Delhi: American Institute of Indian Studies, 1986, pp. 16-44.

Ramanujan, A. K. "Repetition in the *Mahābhārata*." in *Essays on the Mahābhārata*. ed. Arvind Sharma. Leiden: E. J. Brill, 1991, pp. 419-43.

Reich, Tamar. "Sacrificial Violence and Textual Battles: Inner Textual Interpretation in the Sanskrit *Mahābhārata*." *History Of Religions* 41 (2001): 142-69.

Schmidt, Hanns-Peter. "The Origin Of Ahiṃsā." in *Mélanges d'Indianisme à la Mémoire de Louis Renou*. Paris: Editions de Boccard, 1968, pp. 625-55.

Shulman, David. *The Wisdom of Poets: Studies in Tamil, Telegu, and Sanskrit*. Oxford: Oxford UP, 2001.

Sullivan, Bruce M. *Kṛṣṇa Dvaipāyana Vyāsa and the Mahābhārata: A New Interpretation*. Leiden: E. J. Brill, 1990.

Tolstoy, Leo. *War and Peace*. trans. George Gibian. NY: Norton, 1996.

Van Nooten, Barend A. *The Mahābhārata Attributed to Kṛṣṇa Dvaipāyana Vyāsa*. Twayne's World Author Series, 131. NY: Twayne Publishers, 1971.

Woods, Julian F. *Destiny and Human Initiative in the Mahābhārata.* Albany: State U of New York P, 2001.

SASA Books is a project of the South Asian Studies Association, a recognized 501(c)3 non-profit, public benefit corporation of scholars and others interested in South Asia.

Using a *pro bono* model, SASA Books is dedicated to publishing high quality, fully vetted scholarly material. The SASA website is www.sasia.org. SASA Books can be found at www.sasabooks.org.

61065746R00075

Made in the USA
Lexington, KY
27 February 2017